THE COMIC COLLECTION

A GERRY ANDERSON PRODUCTION

THUNDERBIRDS™

EGMONT

This volume first published in Great Britain 2014 by Egmont UK Limited
The Yellow Building, 1 Nicholas Road, London W11 4AN

A GERRY ANDERSON PRODUCTION

Cover illustration by Graham Bleathman

ISBN 978 1 4052 7263 6
56510/1
Printed in Malaysia.

Please note: Some of the comic strips used in this collection
are exceedingly rare, so the print quality may vary.

MIX
Paper from
responsible sources
FSC® C018306

THE COMIC COLLECTION

A GERRY ANDERSON PRODUCTION

THUNDERBIRDS™

VOLUME FOUR

CLASSIC
COMICS

EGMONT

CONTENTS

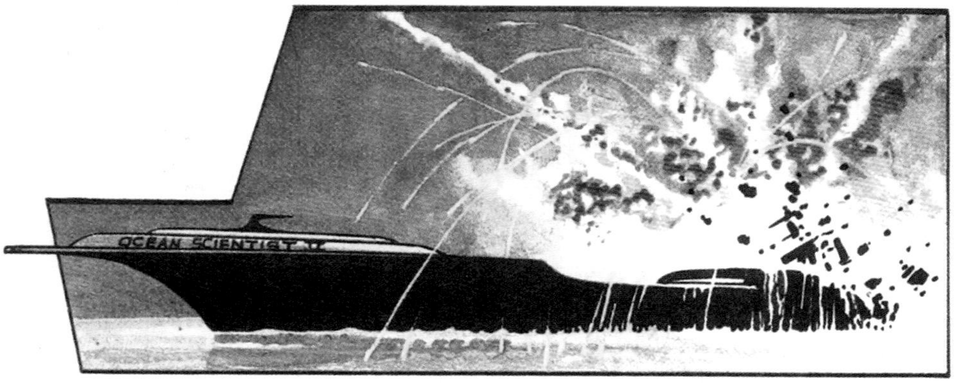

OCEAN SCIENTIST II

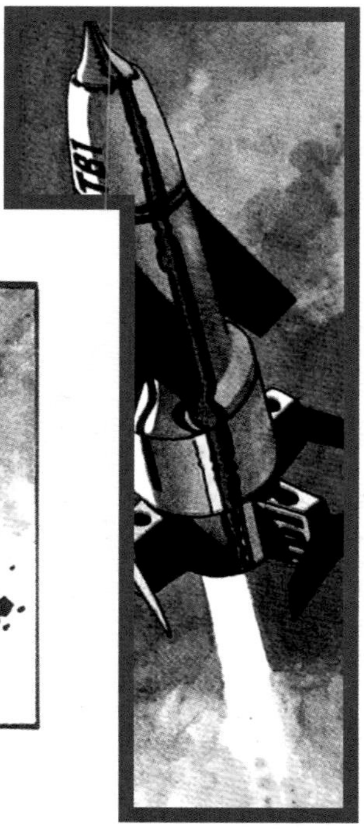

TB1

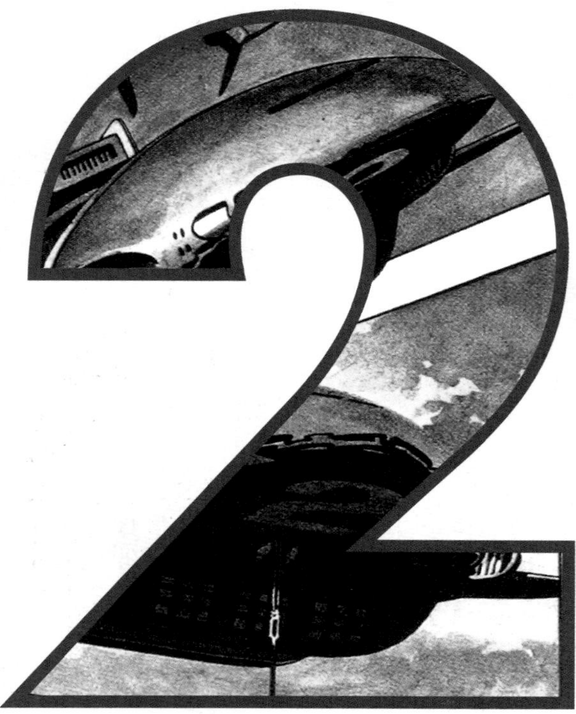

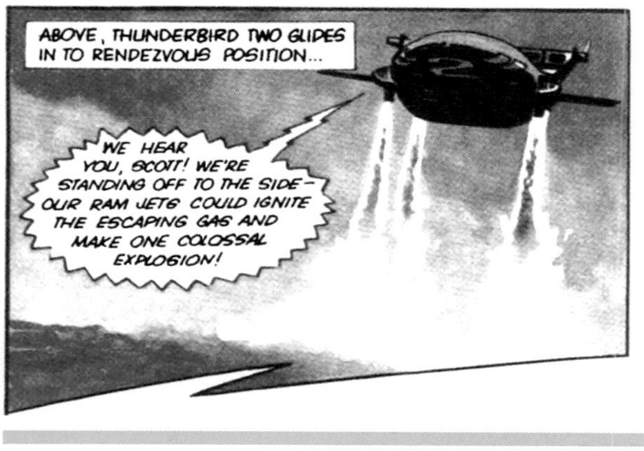

ABOVE, THUNDERBIRD TWO GLIDES IN TO RENDEZVOUS POSITION...
WE HEAR YOU, SCOTT! WE'RE STANDING OFF TO THE SIDE– OUR RAM JETS COULD IGNITE THE ESCAPING GAS AND MAKE ONE COLOSSAL EXPLOSION!

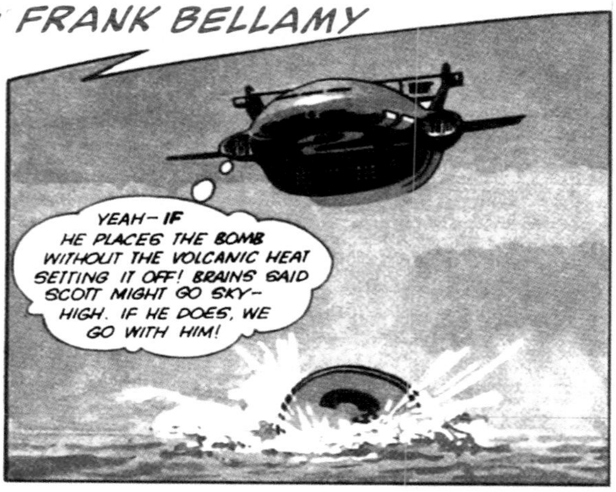

YEAH– IF HE PLACES THE BOMB WITHOUT THE VOLCANIC HEAT SETTING IT OFF! BRAINS SAID SCOTT MIGHT GO SKY-HIGH. IF HE DOES, WE GO WITH HIM!

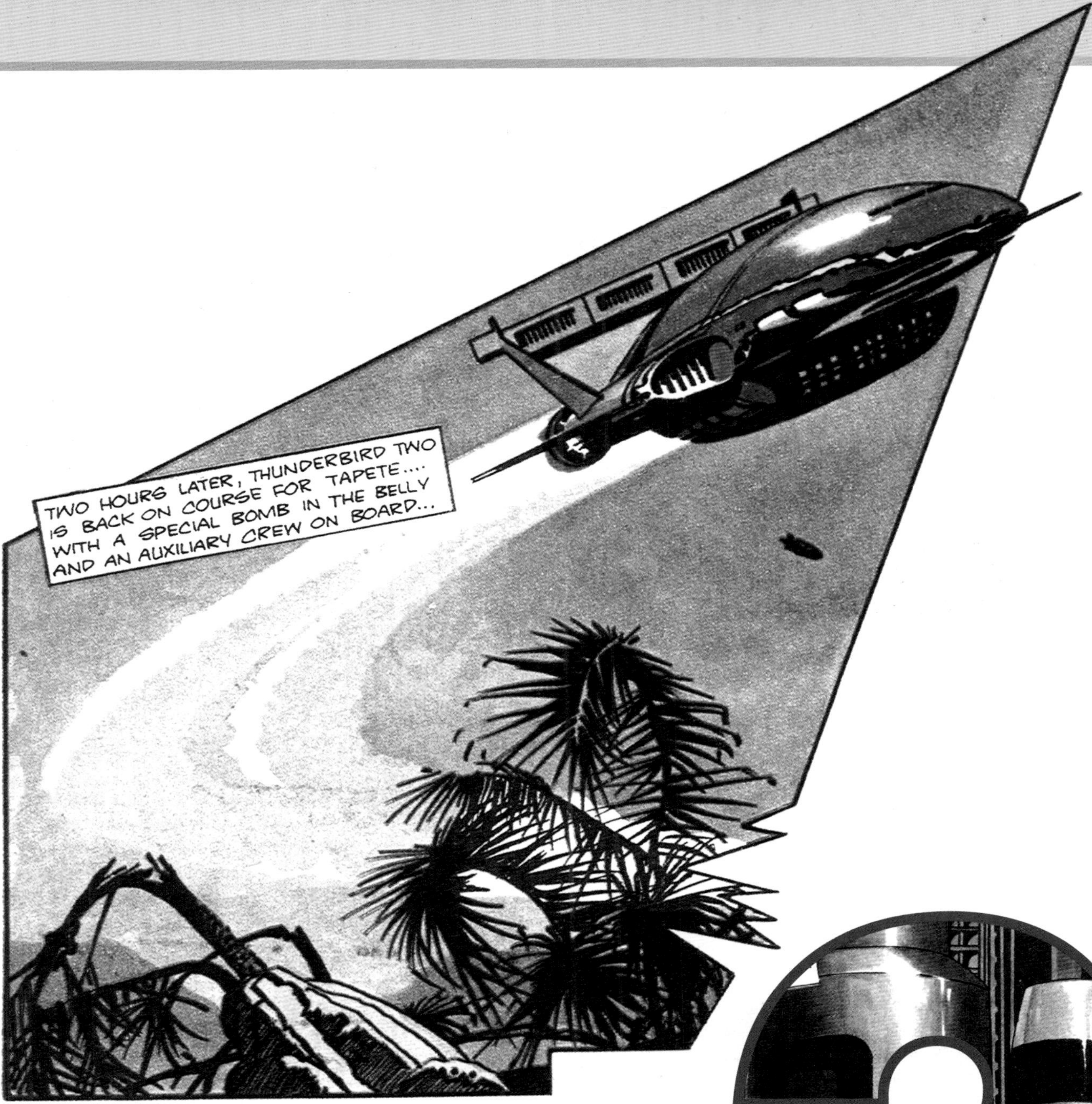
TWO HOURS LATER, THUNDERBIRD TWO IS BACK ON COURSE FOR TAPETE.... WITH A SPECIAL BOMB IN THE BELLY AND AN AUXILIARY CREW ON BOARD...

JUNGLE ADVENTURE..............P40

ARTIST: FRANK BELLAMY

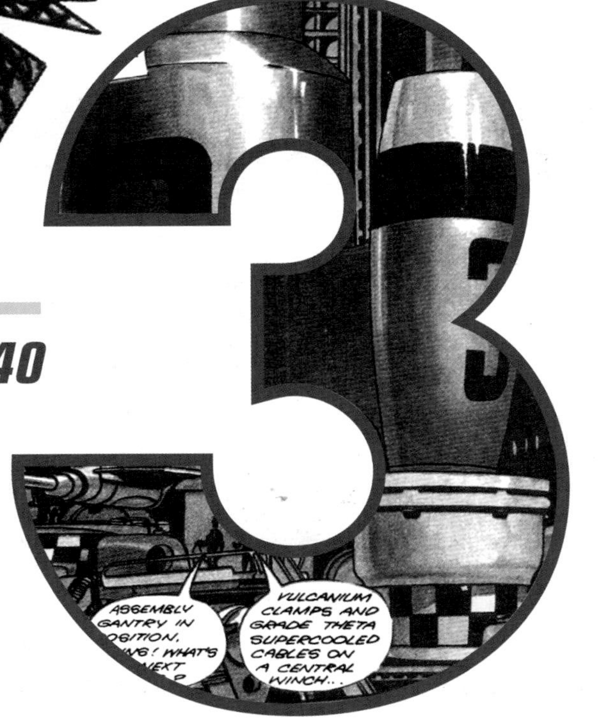
ASSEMBLY GANTRY IN … WHAT'S NEXT
VULCANIUM CLAMPS AND GRADE THETA SUPERCOOLED CABLES ON A CENTRAL WINCH...

Part 1 - dateline 18 January 2069

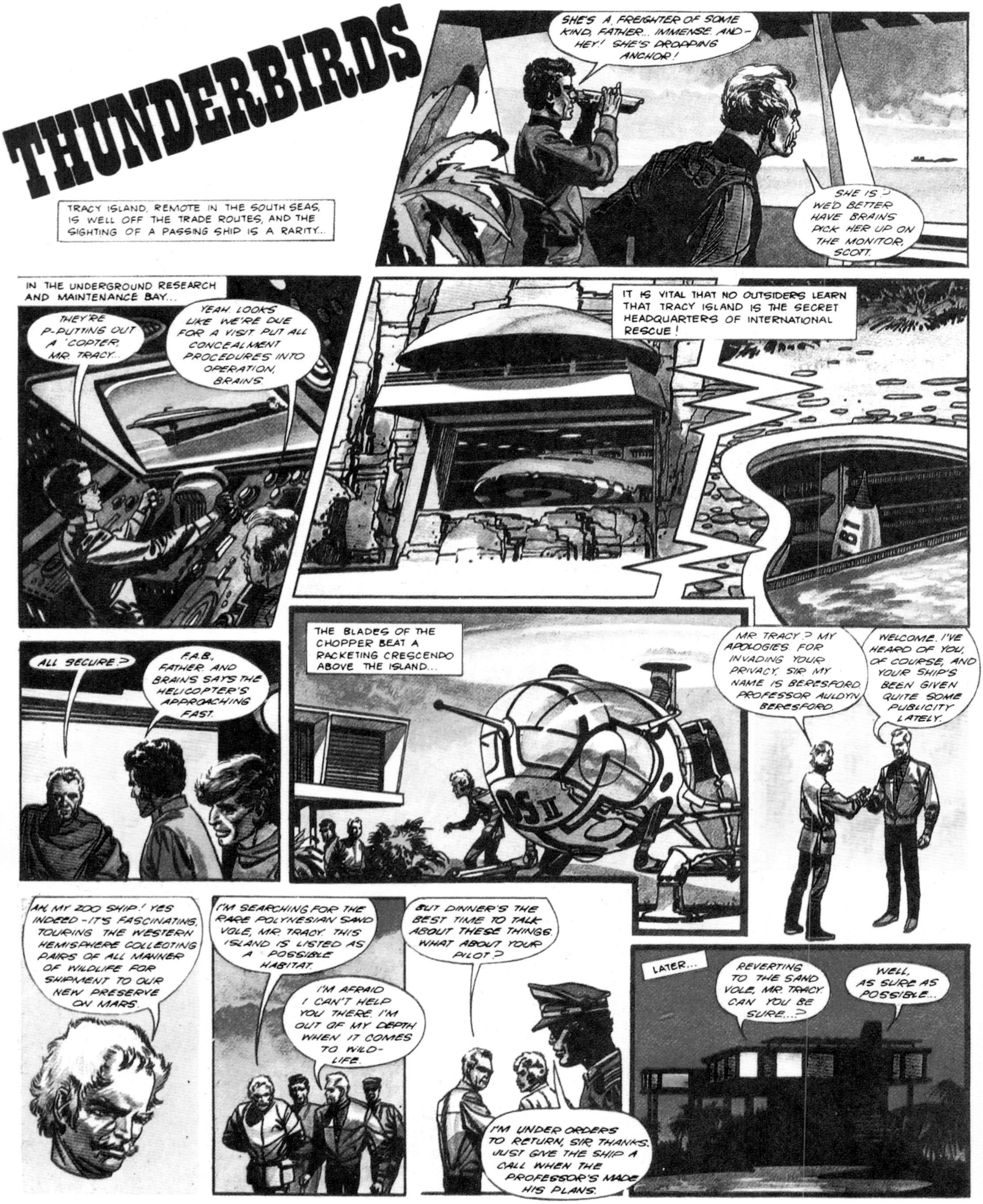
THUNDERBIRDS
TRACY ISLAND, REMOTE IN THE SOUTH SEAS, IS WELL OFF THE TRADE ROUTES, AND THE SIGHTING OF A PASSING SHIP IS A RARITY...
SHE'S A FREIGHTER OF SOME KIND, FATHER... IMMENSE AND - HEY! SHE'S DROPPING ANCHOR!
SHE IS? WE'D BETTER HAVE BRAINS PICK HER UP ON THE MONITOR, SCOTT.
IN THE UNDERGROUND RESEARCH AND MAINTENANCE BAY...
THEY'RE P-PUTTING OUT A 'COPTER, MR. TRACY...
YEAH LOOKS LIKE WE'RE DUE FOR A VISIT. PUT ALL CONCEALMENT PROCEDURES INTO OPERATION, BRAINS.
IT IS VITAL THAT NO OUTSIDERS LEARN THAT TRACY ISLAND IS THE SECRET HEADQUARTERS OF INTERNATIONAL RESCUE!
ALL SECURE?
F.A.B., FATHER AND BRAINS SAYS THE HELICOPTER'S APPROACHING FAST.
THE BLADES OF THE CHOPPER BEAT A RACKETING CRESCENDO ABOVE THE ISLAND...
MR. TRACY? MY APOLOGIES FOR INVADING YOUR PRIVACY, SIR MY NAME IS BERESFORD PROFESSOR AULDYN BERESFORD.
WELCOME. I'VE HEARD OF YOU, OF COURSE, AND YOUR SHIP'S BEEN GIVEN QUITE SOME PUBLICITY LATELY.
AH, MY ZOO SHIP! YES INDEED - IT'S FASCINATING, TOURING THE WESTERN HEMISPHERE COLLECTING PAIRS OF ALL MANNER OF WILDLIFE FOR SHIPMENT TO OUR NEW PRESERVE ON MARS.
I'M SEARCHING FOR THE RARE POLYNESIAN SAND VOLE, MR. TRACY. THIS ISLAND IS LISTED AS A POSSIBLE HABITAT.
I'M AFRAID I CAN'T HELP YOU THERE. I'M OUT OF MY DEPTH WHEN IT COMES TO WILD-LIFE.
BUT DINNER'S THE BEST TIME TO TALK ABOUT THESE THINGS. WHAT ABOUT YOUR PILOT?
I'M UNDER ORDERS TO RETURN, SIR THANKS. JUST GIVE THE SHIP A CALL WHEN THE PROFESSOR'S MADE HIS PLANS.
LATER...
REVERTING TO THE SAND VOLE, MR. TRACY. CAN YOU BE SURE...?
WELL, AS SURE AS POSSIBLE...

Artist: Frank Bellamy

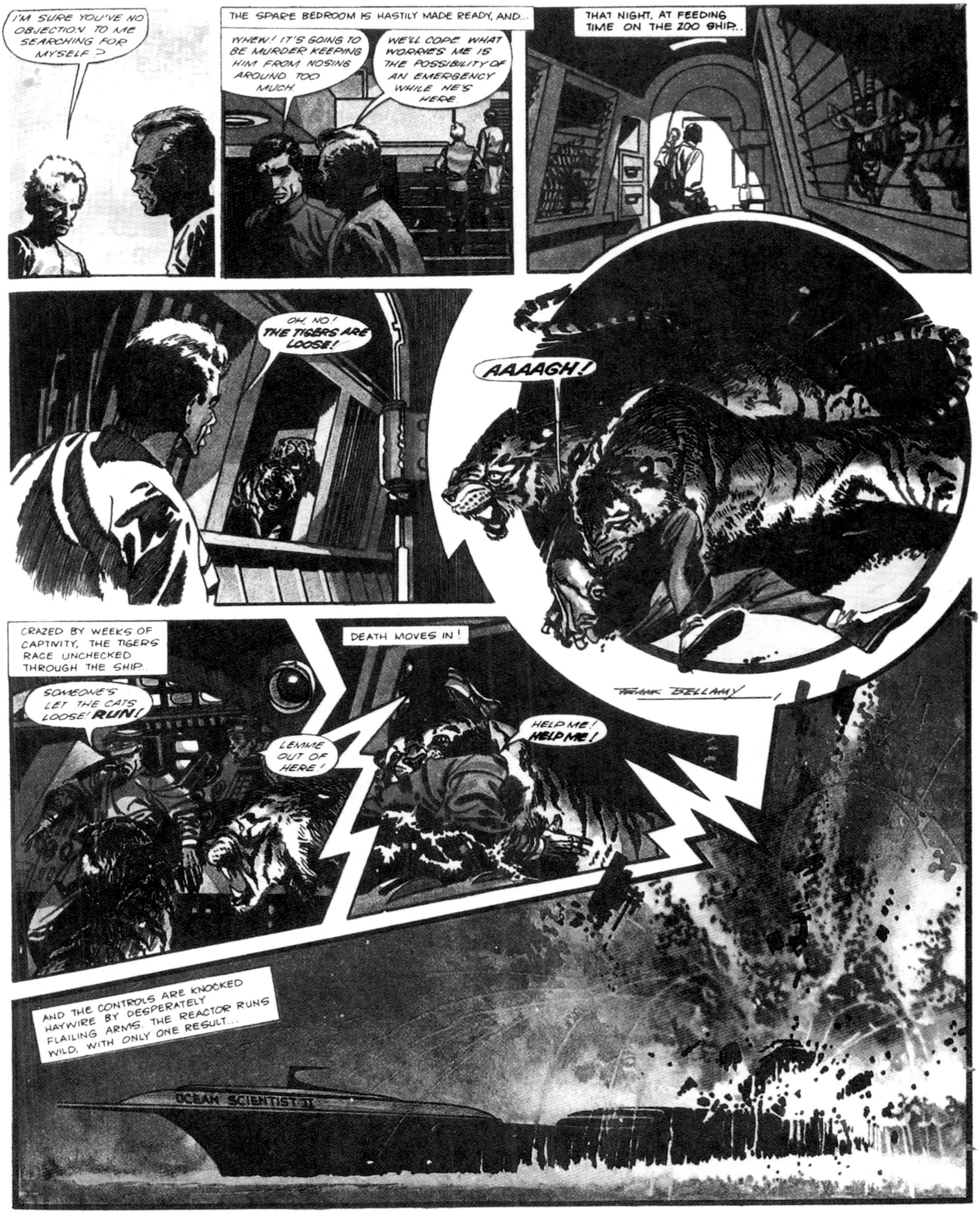

I'M SURE YOU'VE NO OBJECTION TO ME SEARCHING FOR MYSELF?
THE SPARE BEDROOM IS HASTILY MADE READY, AND...
WHEW! IT'S GOING TO BE MURDER KEEPING HIM FROM NOSING AROUND TOO MUCH.
WE'LL COPE. WHAT WORRIES ME IS THE POSSIBILITY OF AN EMERGENCY WHILE HE'S HERE.
THAT NIGHT, AT FEEDING TIME ON THE ZOO SHIP...
OH, NO! THE TIGERS ARE LOOSE!
AAAAGH!
FRANK BELLAMY
CRAZED BY WEEKS OF CAPTIVITY, THE TIGERS RACE UNCHECKED THROUGH THE SHIP...
SOMEONE'S LET THE CATS LOOSE! RUN!
LEMME OUT OF HERE!
DEATH MOVES IN!
HELP ME! HELP ME!
AND THE CONTROLS ARE KNOCKED HAYWIRE BY DESPERATELY FLAILING ARMS. THE REACTOR RUNS WILD, WITH ONLY ONE RESULT...
OCEAN SCIENTIST II

Part 2 - dateline 25 January 2069

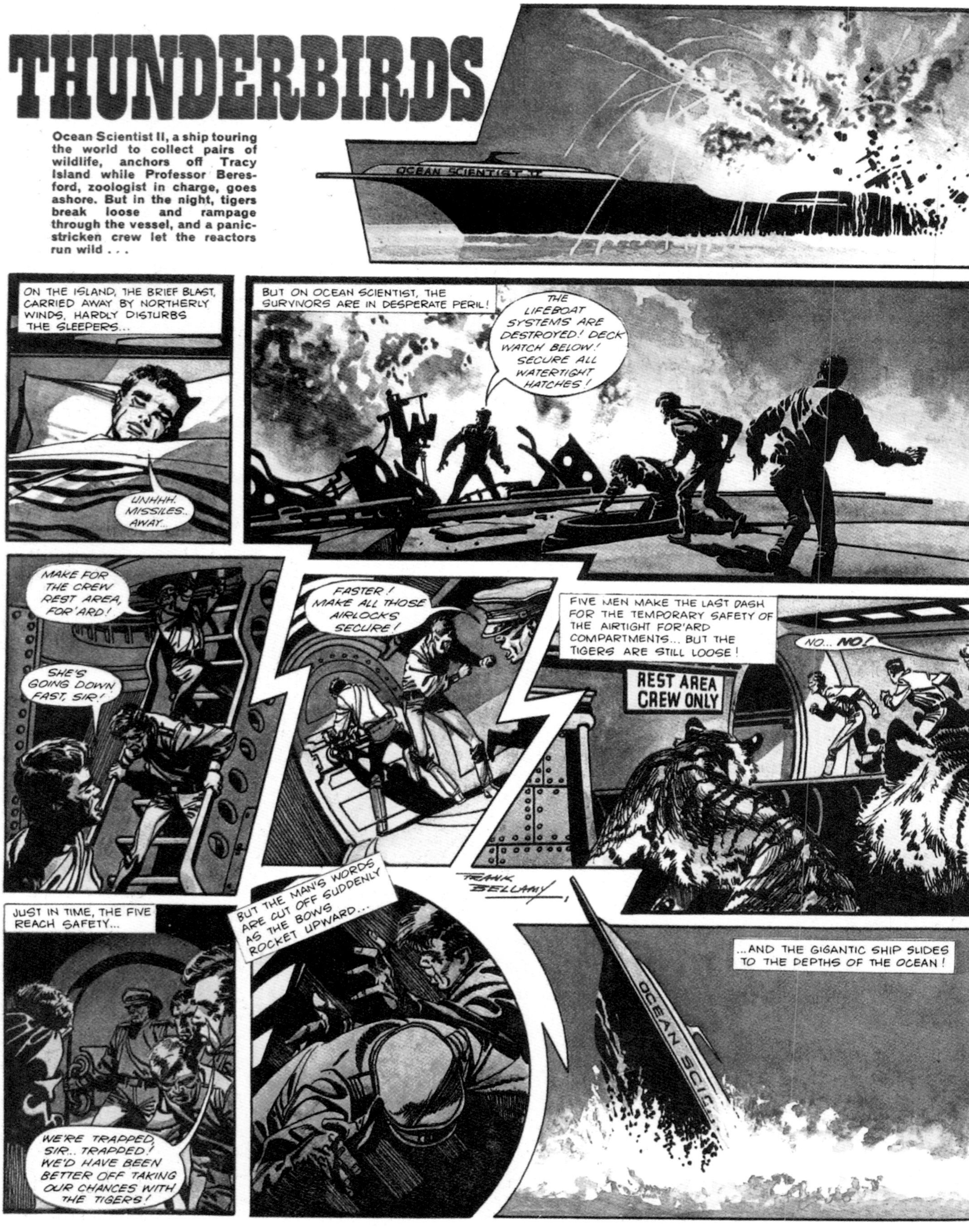
THUNDERBIRDS
Ocean Scientist II, a ship touring the world to collect pairs of wildlife, anchors off Tracy Island while Professor Beresford, zoologist in charge, goes ashore. But in the night, tigers break loose and rampage through the vessel, and a panic-stricken crew let the reactors run wild . . .
OCEAN SCIENTIST II
ON THE ISLAND, THE BRIEF BLAST, CARRIED AWAY BY NORTHERLY WINDS, HARDLY DISTURBS THE SLEEPERS...
UNHHH. MISSILES.. AWAY...
BUT ON OCEAN SCIENTIST, THE SURVIVORS ARE IN DESPERATE PERIL!
THE LIFEBOAT SYSTEMS ARE DESTROYED! DECK WATCH BELOW! SECURE ALL WATERTIGHT HATCHES!
MAKE FOR THE CREW REST AREA, FOR'ARD!
SHE'S GOING DOWN FAST, SIR!
FASTER! MAKE ALL THOSE AIRLOCKS SECURE!
FIVE MEN MAKE THE LAST DASH FOR THE TEMPORARY SAFETY OF THE AIRTIGHT FOR'ARD COMPARTMENTS... BUT THE TIGERS ARE STILL LOOSE!
NO... NO!
REST AREA CREW ONLY
FRANK BELLAMY
JUST IN TIME, THE FIVE REACH SAFETY...
WE'RE TRAPPED, SIR... TRAPPED! WE'D HAVE BEEN BETTER OFF TAKING OUR CHANCES WITH THE TIGERS!
BUT THE MAN'S WORDS ARE CUT OFF SUDDENLY AS THE BOWS ROCKET UPWARD...
...AND THE GIGANTIC SHIP SLIDES TO THE DEPTHS OF THE OCEAN!
OCEAN SCI

Artist: Frank Bellamy

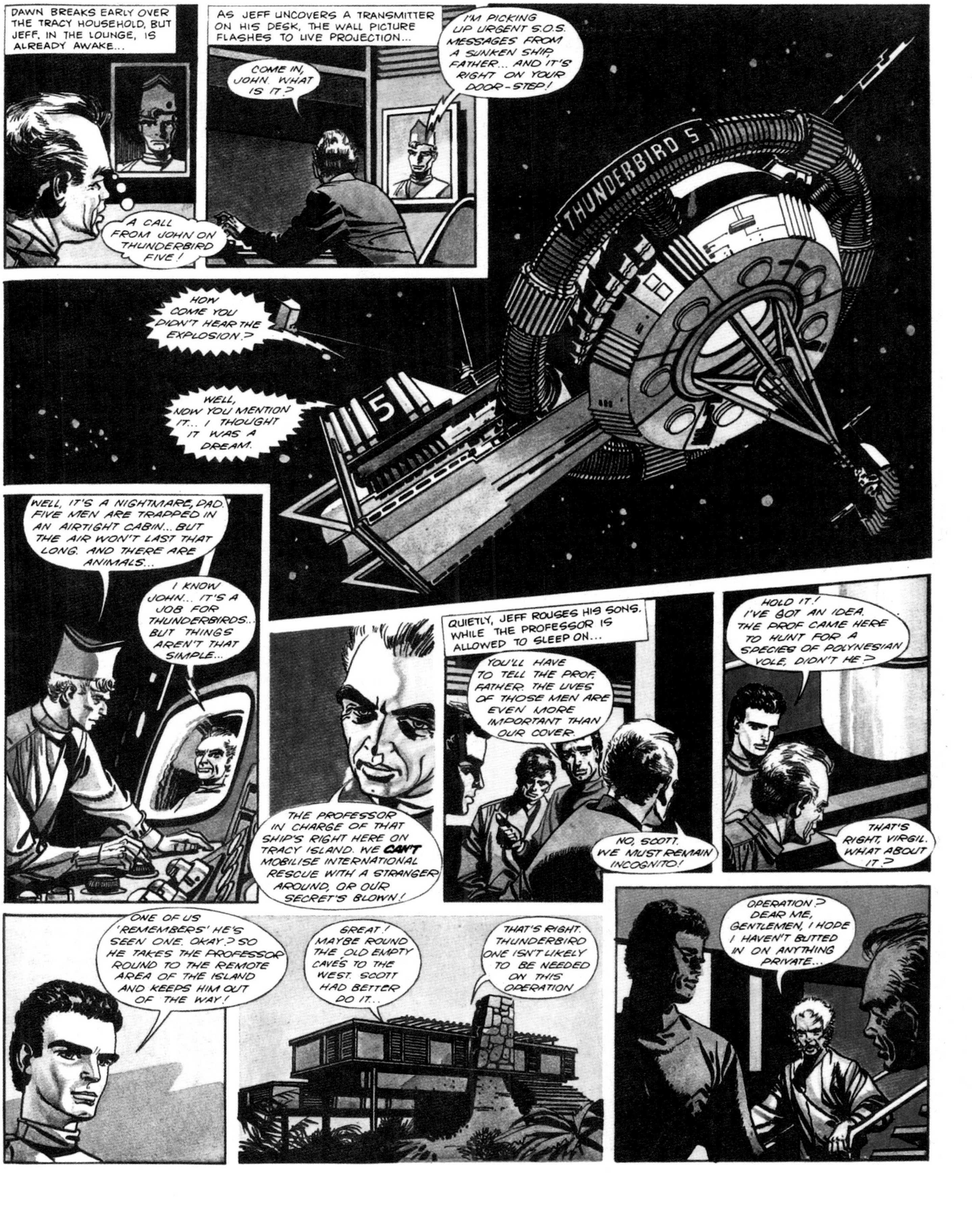
DAWN BREAKS EARLY OVER THE TRACY HOUSEHOLD, BUT JEFF, IN THE LOUNGE, IS ALREADY AWAKE...
A CALL FROM JOHN ON THUNDERBIRD FIVE!
AS JEFF UNCOVERS A TRANSMITTER ON HIS DESK, THE WALL PICTURE FLASHES TO LIVE PROJECTION...
COME IN, JOHN. WHAT IS IT?
I'M PICKING UP URGENT S.O.S. MESSAGES FROM A SUNKEN SHIP, FATHER... AND IT'S RIGHT ON YOUR DOOR-STEP!
THUNDERBIRD 5
HOW COME YOU DIDN'T HEAR THE EXPLOSION?
WELL, NOW YOU MENTION IT... I THOUGHT IT WAS A DREAM.
WELL, IT'S A NIGHTMARE, DAD. FIVE MEN ARE TRAPPED IN AN AIRTIGHT CABIN... BUT THE AIR WON'T LAST THAT LONG. AND THERE ARE ANIMALS...
I KNOW JOHN... IT'S A JOB FOR THUNDERBIRDS... BUT THINGS AREN'T THAT SIMPLE...
THE PROFESSOR IN CHARGE OF THAT SHIP'S RIGHT HERE ON TRACY ISLAND. WE CAN'T MOBILISE INTERNATIONAL RESCUE WITH A STRANGER AROUND, OR OUR SECRET'S BLOWN!
QUIETLY, JEFF ROUSES HIS SONS, WHILE THE PROFESSOR IS ALLOWED TO SLEEP ON...
YOU'LL HAVE TO TELL THE PROF, FATHER. THE LIVES OF THOSE MEN ARE EVEN MORE IMPORTANT THAN OUR COVER.
NO, SCOTT. WE MUST REMAIN INCOGNITO!
HOLD IT! I'VE GOT AN IDEA. THE PROF CAME HERE TO HUNT FOR A SPECIES OF POLYNESIAN VOLE, DIDN'T HE?
THAT'S RIGHT, VIRGIL. WHAT ABOUT IT?
ONE OF US 'REMEMBERS' HE'S SEEN ONE. OKAY? SO HE TAKES THE PROFESSOR ROUND TO THE REMOTE AREA OF THE ISLAND AND KEEPS HIM OUT OF THE WAY!
GREAT! MAYBE ROUND THE OLD EMPTY CAVES TO THE WEST. SCOTT HAD BETTER DO IT...
THAT'S RIGHT. THUNDERBIRD ONE ISN'T LIKELY TO BE NEEDED ON THIS OPERATION
OPERATION? DEAR ME, GENTLEMEN, I HOPE I HAVEN'T BUTTED IN ON ANYTHING PRIVATE...

Part 3 - dateline 01 February 2069

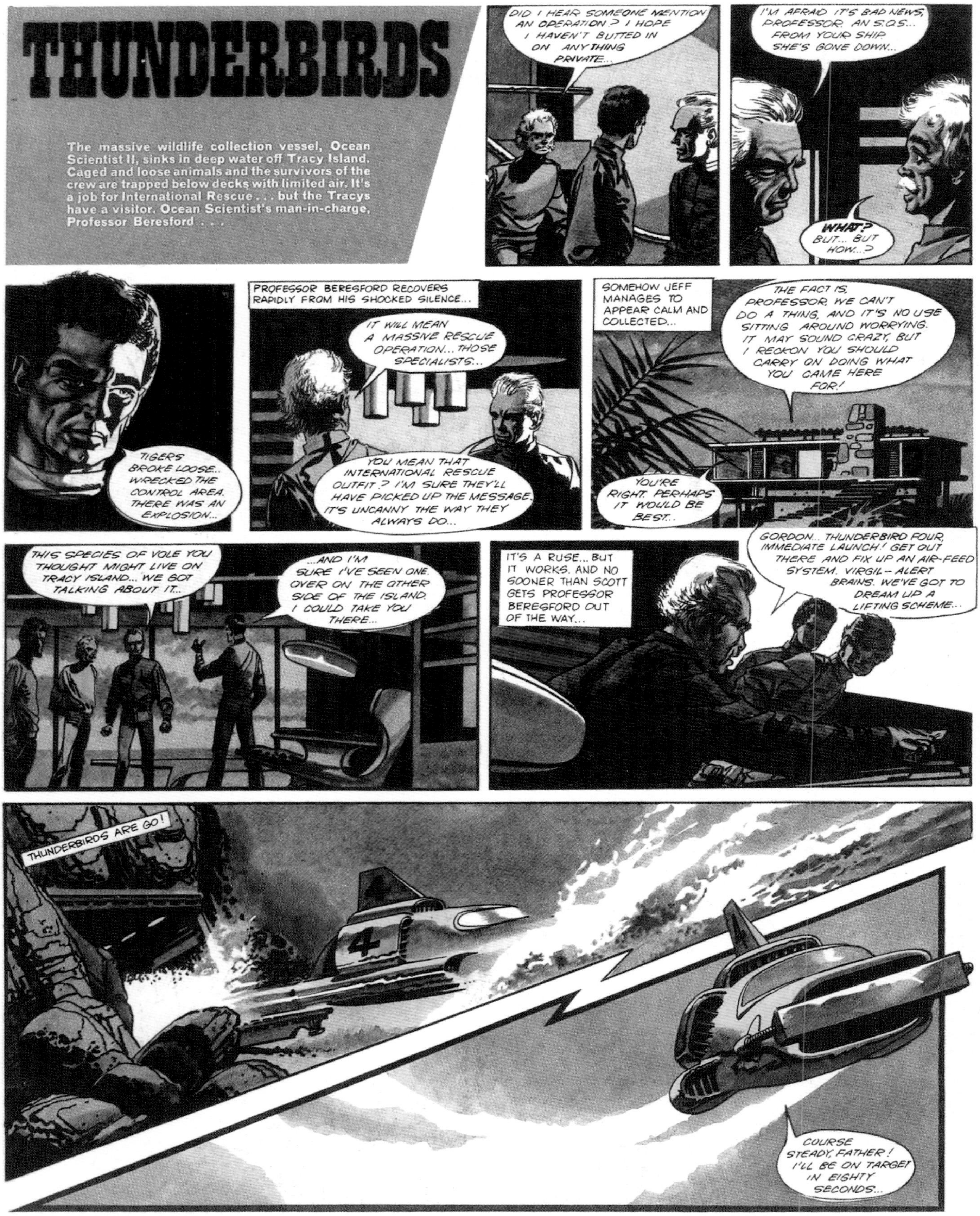
THUNDERBIRDS
The massive wildlife collection vessel, Ocean Scientist II, sinks in deep water off Tracy Island. Caged and loose animals and the survivors of the crew are trapped below decks with limited air. It's a job for International Rescue . . . but the Tracys have a visitor. Ocean Scientist's man-in-charge, Professor Beresford . . .
DID I HEAR SOMEONE MENTION AN OPERATION? I HOPE I HAVEN'T BUTTED IN ON ANYTHING PRIVATE...
I'M AFRAID IT'S BAD NEWS, PROFESSOR. AN S.O.S... FROM YOUR SHIP. SHE'S GONE DOWN...
WHAT? BUT... BUT HOW...?
TIGERS BROKE LOOSE... WRECKED THE CONTROL AREA. THERE WAS AN EXPLOSION...
PROFESSOR BERESFORD RECOVERS RAPIDLY FROM HIS SHOCKED SILENCE...
IT WILL MEAN A MASSIVE RESCUE OPERATION... THOSE SPECIALISTS...
YOU MEAN THAT INTERNATIONAL RESCUE OUTFIT? I'M SURE THEY'LL HAVE PICKED UP THE MESSAGE. IT'S UNCANNY THE WAY THEY ALWAYS DO...
SOMEHOW JEFF MANAGES TO APPEAR CALM AND COLLECTED...
THE FACT IS, PROFESSOR, WE CAN'T DO A THING, AND IT'S NO USE SITTING AROUND WORRYING. IT MAY SOUND CRAZY, BUT I RECKON YOU SHOULD CARRY ON DOING WHAT YOU CAME HERE FOR!
YOU'RE RIGHT. PERHAPS IT WOULD BE BEST...
THIS SPECIES OF VOLE YOU THOUGHT MIGHT LIVE ON TRACY ISLAND... WE GOT TALKING ABOUT IT...
...AND I'M SURE I'VE SEEN ONE. OVER ON THE OTHER SIDE OF THE ISLAND. I COULD TAKE YOU THERE...
IT'S A RUSE... BUT IT WORKS. AND NO SOONER THAN SCOTT GETS PROFESSOR BERESFORD OUT OF THE WAY...
GORDON... THUNDERBIRD FOUR, IMMEDIATE LAUNCH! GET OUT THERE AND FIX UP AN AIR-FEED SYSTEM. VIRGIL – ALERT BRAINS. WE'VE GOT TO DREAM UP A LIFTING SCHEME...
THUNDERBIRDS ARE GO!
COURSE STEADY, FATHER! I'LL BE ON TARGET IN EIGHTY SECONDS...

Artist: Frank Bellamy

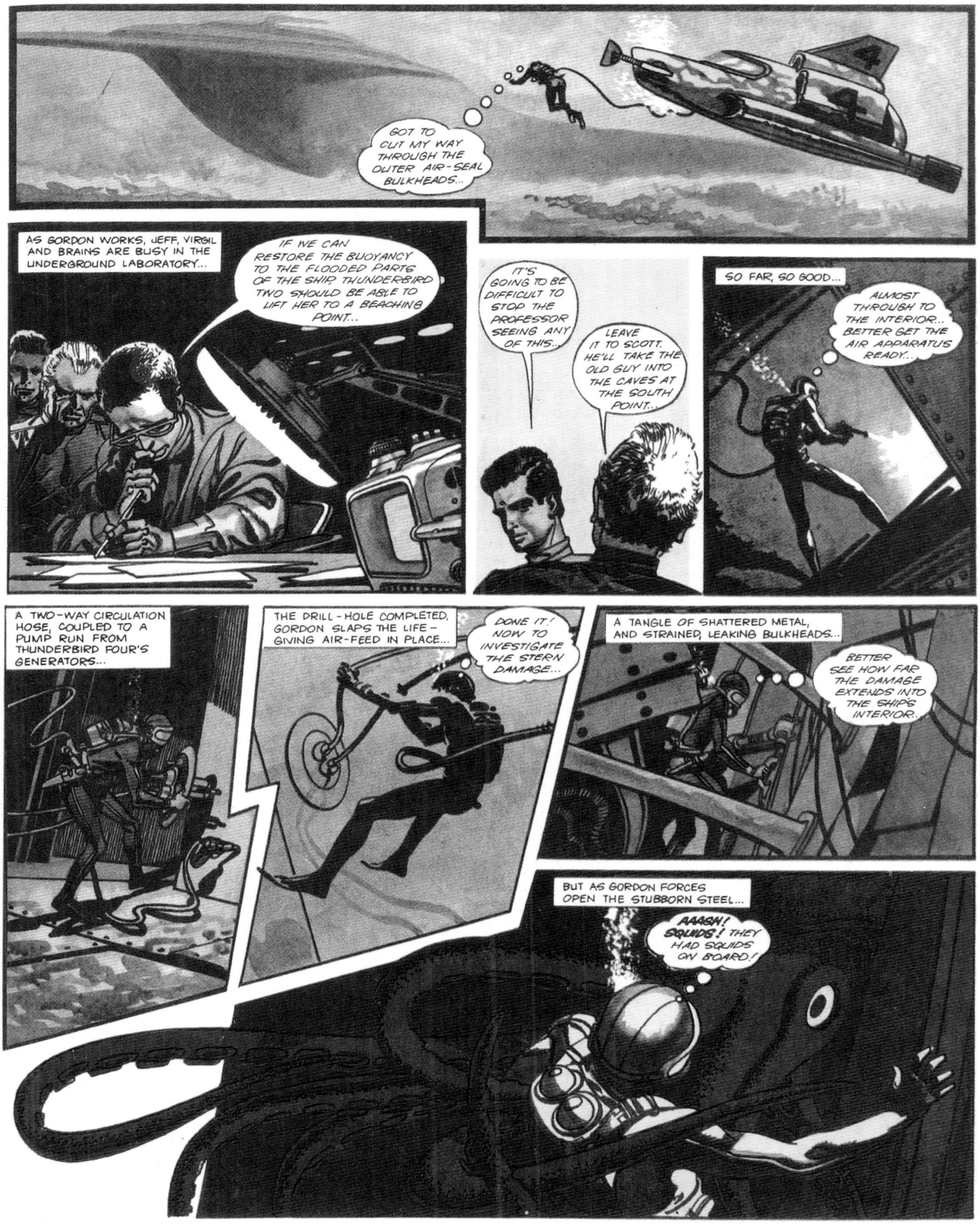
GOT TO CUT MY WAY THROUGH THE OUTER AIR-SEAL BULKHEADS...
AS GORDON WORKS, JEFF, VIRGIL AND BRAINS ARE BUSY IN THE UNDERGROUND LABORATORY...
IF WE CAN RESTORE THE BUOYANCY TO THE FLOODED PARTS OF THE SHIP, THUNDERBIRD TWO SHOULD BE ABLE TO LIFT HER TO A BEACHING POINT...
IT'S GOING TO BE DIFFICULT TO STOP THE PROFESSOR SEEING ANY OF THIS...
LEAVE IT TO SCOTT. HE'LL TAKE THE OLD GUY INTO THE CAVES AT THE SOUTH POINT...
SO FAR, SO GOOD...
ALMOST THROUGH TO THE INTERIOR... BETTER GET THE AIR APPARATUS READY...
A TWO-WAY CIRCULATION HOSE, COUPLED TO A PUMP RUN FROM THUNDERBIRD FOUR'S GENERATORS...
THE DRILL-HOLE COMPLETED, GORDON SLAPS THE LIFE-GIVING AIR-FEED IN PLACE...
DONE IT! NOW TO INVESTIGATE THE STERN DAMAGE...
A TANGLE OF SHATTERED METAL, AND STRAINED, LEAKING BULKHEADS...
BETTER SEE HOW FAR THE DAMAGE EXTENDS INTO THE SHIP'S INTERIOR...
BUT AS GORDON FORCES OPEN THE STUBBORN STEEL...
AAAGH! SQUIDS! THEY HAD SQUIDS ON BOARD!

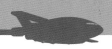

Part 4 - dateline 08 February 2069

THUNDERBIRDS

Ocean Scientist II, a huge wildlife collection vessel, sinks off Tracy Island, trapping crew and animals inside. Ashore on the island, the ship's zoologist Professor Beresford, is diverted by Scott Tracy while International Rescue swings into action . . . But Gordon finds unexpected danger in the sunken ship!

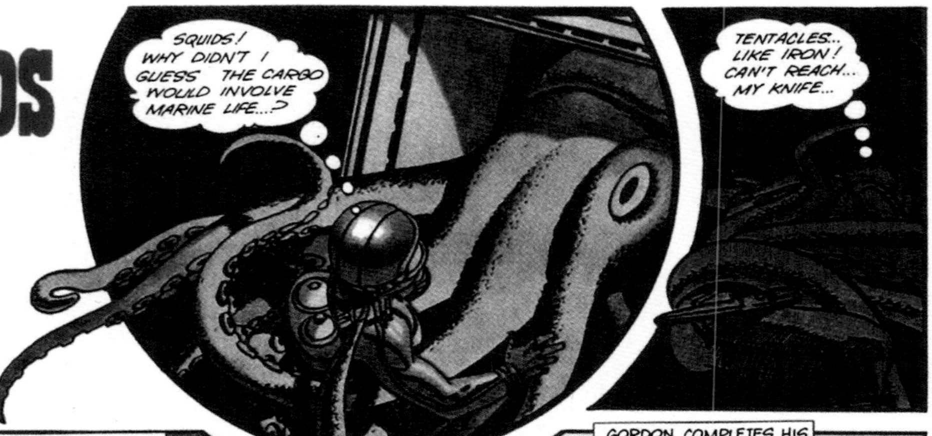
SQUIDS! WHY DIDN'T I GUESS THE CARGO WOULD INVOLVE MARINE LIFE...?
TENTACLES... LIKE IRON! CAN'T REACH... MY KNIFE...

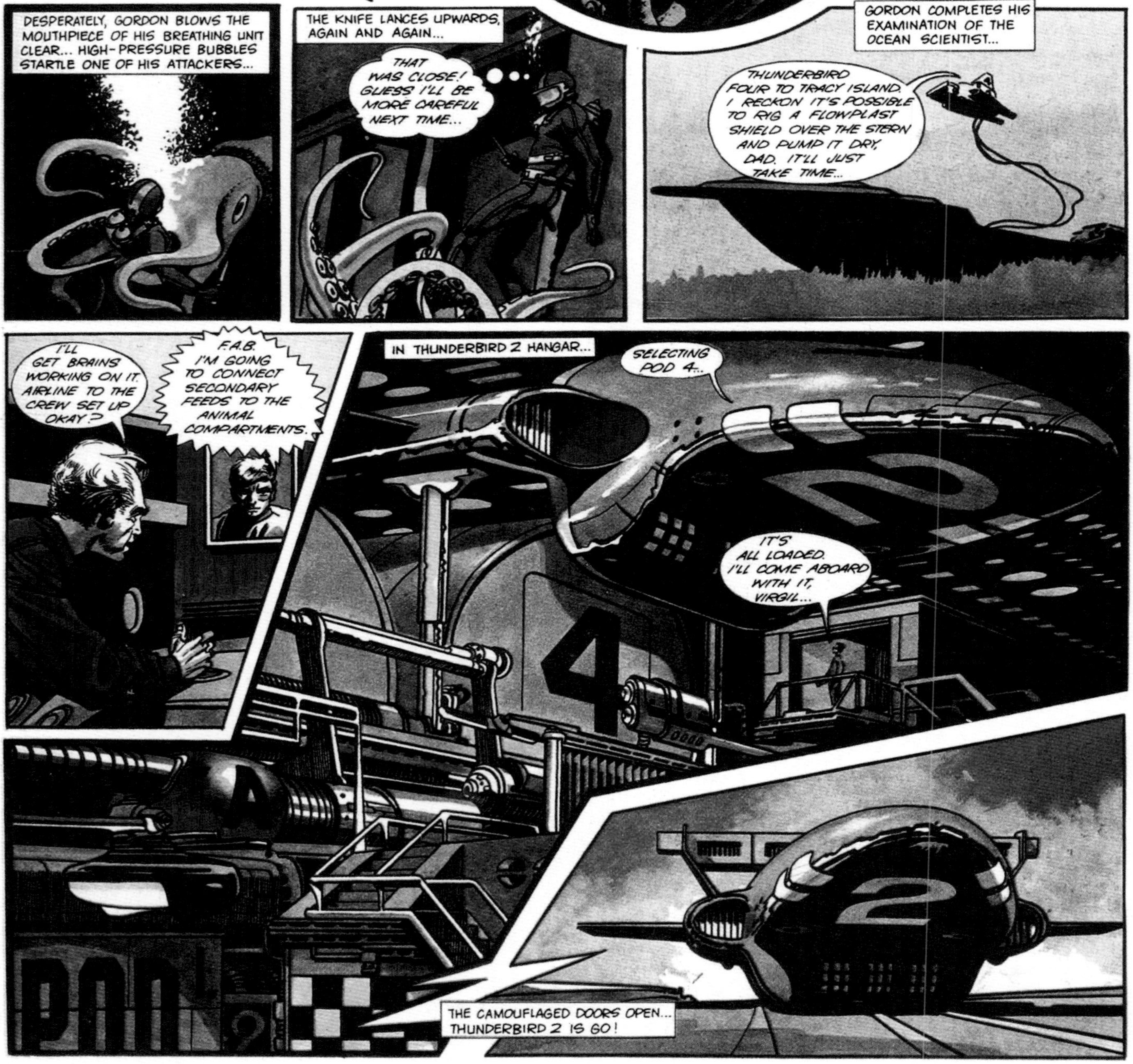
DESPERATELY, GORDON BLOWS THE MOUTHPIECE OF HIS BREATHING UNIT CLEAR... HIGH-PRESSURE BUBBLES STARTLE ONE OF HIS ATTACKERS...
THE KNIFE LANCES UPWARDS, AGAIN AND AGAIN...
THAT WAS CLOSE! GUESS I'LL BE MORE CAREFUL NEXT TIME...
GORDON COMPLETES HIS EXAMINATION OF THE OCEAN SCIENTIST...
THUNDERBIRD FOUR TO TRACY ISLAND. I RECKON IT'S POSSIBLE TO RIG A FLOWPLAST SHIELD OVER THE STERN AND PUMP IT DRY, DAD. IT'LL JUST TAKE TIME...
I'LL GET BRAINS WORKING ON IT. AIRLINE TO THE CREW SET UP OKAY?
F.A.B. I'M GOING TO CONNECT SECONDARY FEEDS TO THE ANIMAL COMPARTMENTS.
IN THUNDERBIRD 2 HANGAR...
SELECTING POD 4...
IT'S ALL LOADED. I'LL COME ABOARD WITH IT, VIRGIL...
THE CAMOUFLAGED DOORS OPEN... THUNDERBIRD 2 IS GO!

Artist: Frank Bellamy

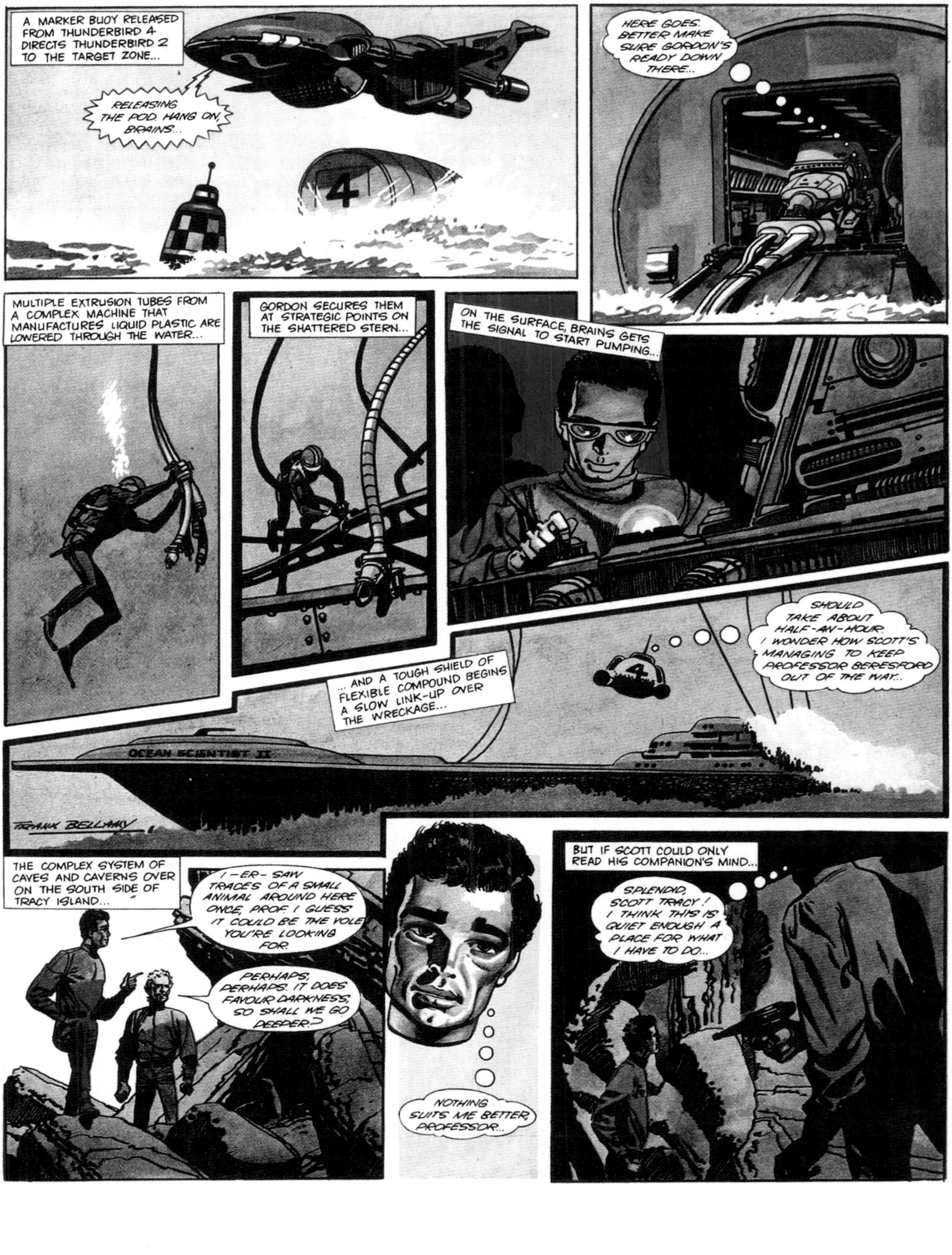
A MARKER BUOY RELEASED FROM THUNDERBIRD 4 DIRECTS THUNDERBIRD 2 TO THE TARGET ZONE...
RELEASING THE POD. HANG ON, BRAINS...
HERE GOES. BETTER MAKE SURE GORDON'S READY DOWN THERE...
MULTIPLE EXTRUSION TUBES FROM A COMPLEX MACHINE THAT MANUFACTURES LIQUID PLASTIC ARE LOWERED THROUGH THE WATER...
GORDON SECURES THEM AT STRATEGIC POINTS ON THE SHATTERED STERN...
ON THE SURFACE, BRAINS GETS THE SIGNAL TO START PUMPING...
SHOULD TAKE ABOUT HALF-AN-HOUR. I WONDER HOW SCOTT'S MANAGING TO KEEP PROFESSOR BERESFORD OUT OF THE WAY...
... AND A TOUGH SHIELD OF FLEXIBLE COMPOUND BEGINS A SLOW LINK-UP OVER THE WRECKAGE...
OCEAN SCIENTIST II
FRANK BELLAMY
THE COMPLEX SYSTEM OF CAVES AND CAVERNS OVER ON THE SOUTH SIDE OF TRACY ISLAND...
I -ER- SAW TRACES OF A SMALL ANIMAL AROUND HERE ONCE, PROF. I GUESS IT COULD BE THE VOLE YOU'RE LOOKING FOR.
PERHAPS, PERHAPS. IT DOES FAVOUR DARKNESS, SO SHALL WE GO DEEPER?
NOTHING SUITS ME BETTER, PROFESSOR...
BUT IF SCOTT COULD ONLY READ HIS COMPANION'S MIND...
SPLENDID, SCOTT TRACY! I THINK THIS IS QUIET ENOUGH A PLACE FOR WHAT I HAVE TO DO...

Part 5 - dateline 15 February 2069

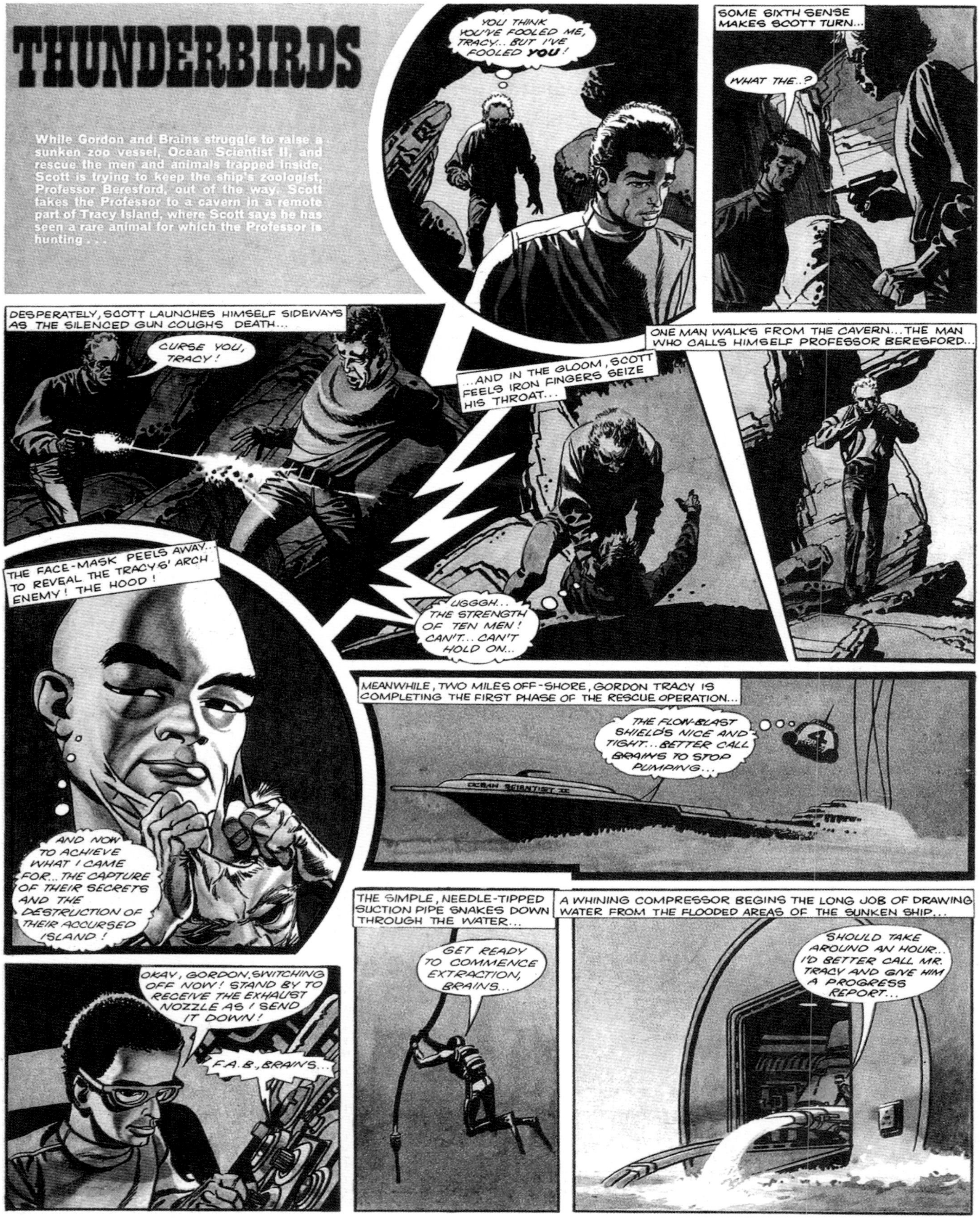
THUNDERBIRDS
While Gordon and Brains struggle to raise a sunken zoo vessel, Ocean Scientist II, and rescue the men and animals trapped inside, Scott is trying to keep the ship's zoologist, Professor Beresford, out of the way. Scott takes the Professor to a cavern in a remote part of Tracy Island, where Scott says he has seen a rare animal for which the Professor is hunting . . .
YOU THINK YOU'VE FOOLED ME, TRACY... BUT I'VE FOOLED YOU!
SOME SIXTH SENSE MAKES SCOTT TURN...
WHAT THE..?
DESPERATELY, SCOTT LAUNCHES HIMSELF SIDEWAYS AS THE SILENCED GUN COUGHS DEATH...
CURSE YOU, TRACY!
...AND IN THE GLOOM, SCOTT FEELS IRON FINGERS SEIZE HIS THROAT...
UGGGH... THE STRENGTH OF TEN MEN! CAN'T... CAN'T HOLD ON...
ONE MAN WALKS FROM THE CAVERN... THE MAN WHO CALLS HIMSELF PROFESSOR BERESFORD...
THE FACE-MASK PEELS AWAY... TO REVEAL THE TRACYS' ARCH ENEMY! THE HOOD!
AND NOW TO ACHIEVE WHAT I CAME FOR... THE CAPTURE OF THEIR SECRETS AND THE DESTRUCTION OF THEIR ACCURSED ISLAND!
MEANWHILE, TWO MILES OFF-SHORE, GORDON TRACY IS COMPLETING THE FIRST PHASE OF THE RESCUE OPERATION...
THE FLOW-BLAST SHIELD'S NICE AND TIGHT... BETTER CALL BRAINS TO STOP PUMPING...
OCEAN SCIENTIST II
OKAY, GORDON, SWITCHING OFF NOW! STAND BY TO RECEIVE THE EXHAUST NOZZLE AS I SEND IT DOWN!
F.A.B., BRAINS...
THE SIMPLE, NEEDLE-TIPPED SUCTION PIPE SNAKES DOWN THROUGH THE WATER...
GET READY TO COMMENCE EXTRACTION, BRAINS...
A WHINING COMPRESSOR BEGINS THE LONG JOB OF DRAWING WATER FROM THE FLOODED AREAS OF THE SUNKEN SHIP...
SHOULD TAKE AROUND AN HOUR... I'D BETTER CALL MR. TRACY AND GIVE HIM A PROGRESS REPORT...

Artist: Frank Bellamy

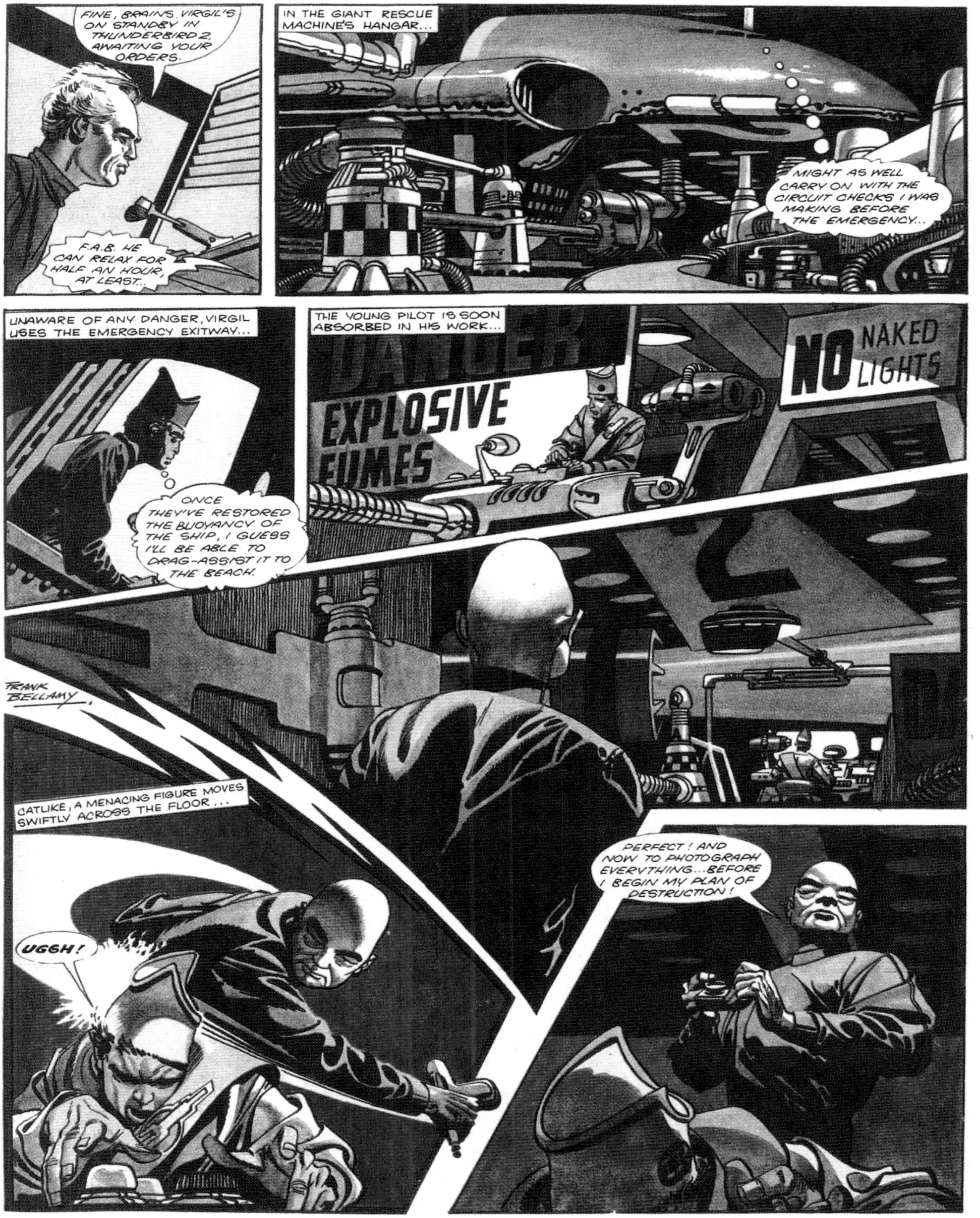
FINE, BRAINS. VIRGIL'S ON STANDBY IN THUNDERBIRD 2, AWAITING YOUR ORDERS.
F.A.B. HE CAN RELAX FOR HALF AN HOUR, AT LEAST...
IN THE GIANT RESCUE MACHINE'S HANGAR...
MIGHT AS WELL CARRY ON WITH THE CIRCUIT CHECKS I WAS MAKING BEFORE THE EMERGENCY...
UNAWARE OF ANY DANGER, VIRGIL USES THE EMERGENCY EXITWAY...
ONCE THEY'VE RESTORED THE BUOYANCY OF THE SHIP, I GUESS I'LL BE ABLE TO DRAG-ASSIST IT TO THE BEACH.
THE YOUNG PILOT IS SOON ABSORBED IN HIS WORK...
DANGER
EXPLOSIVE FUMES
NO NAKED LIGHTS
FRANK BELLAMY
CATLIKE, A MENACING FIGURE MOVES SWIFTLY ACROSS THE FLOOR...
UGGH!
PERFECT! AND NOW TO PHOTOGRAPH EVERYTHING...BEFORE I BEGIN MY PLAN OF DESTRUCTION!

Part 6 - dateline 22 February 2069

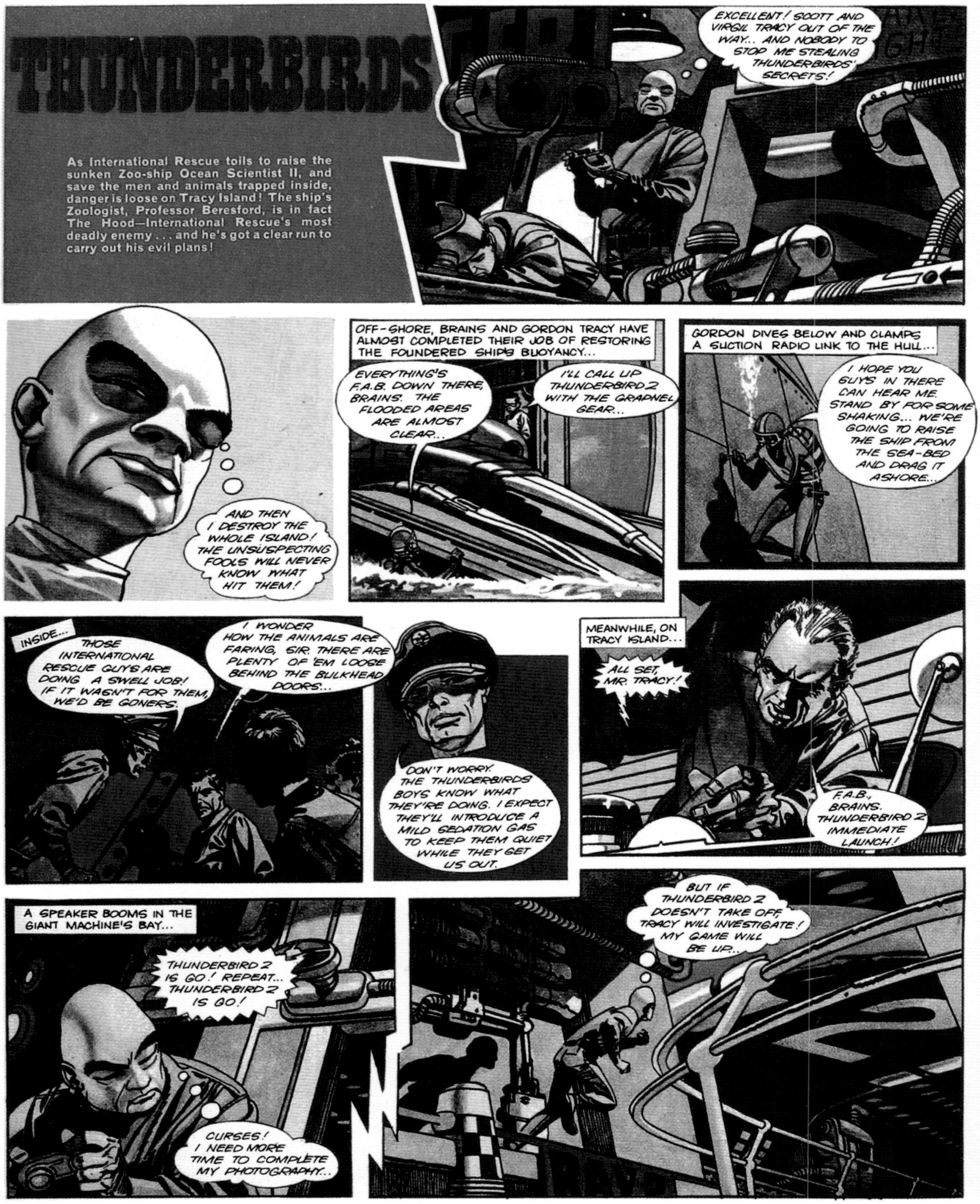
THUNDERBIRDS
As International Rescue toils to raise the sunken Zoo-ship Ocean Scientist II, and save the men and animals trapped inside, danger is loose on Tracy Island! The ship's Zoologist, Professor Beresford, is in fact The Hood—International Rescue's most deadly enemy . . . and he's got a clear run to carry out his evil plans!
EXCELLENT! SCOTT AND VIRGIL TRACY OUT OF THE WAY... AND NOBODY TO STOP ME STEALING THUNDERBIRDS' SECRETS!
AND THEN I DESTROY THE WHOLE ISLAND! THE UNSUSPECTING FOOLS WILL NEVER KNOW WHAT HIT THEM!
OFF-SHORE, BRAINS AND GORDON TRACY HAVE ALMOST COMPLETED THEIR JOB OF RESTORING THE FOUNDERED SHIP'S BUOYANCY...
EVERYTHING'S F.A.B. DOWN THERE, BRAINS. THE FLOODED AREAS ARE ALMOST CLEAR...
I'LL CALL UP THUNDERBIRD 2 WITH THE GRAPNEL GEAR...
GORDON DIVES BELOW AND CLAMPS A SUCTION RADIO LINK TO THE HULL...
I HOPE YOU GUYS IN THERE CAN HEAR ME. STAND BY FOR SOME SHAKING... WE'RE GOING TO RAISE THE SHIP FROM THE SEA-BED AND DRAG IT ASHORE...
INSIDE...
THOSE INTERNATIONAL RESCUE GUYS ARE DOING A SWELL JOB! IF IT WASN'T FOR THEM, WE'D BE GONERS.
I WONDER HOW THE ANIMALS ARE FARING, SIR. THERE ARE PLENTY OF 'EM LOOSE BEHIND THE BULKHEAD DOORS...
DON'T WORRY. THE THUNDERBIRDS BOYS KNOW WHAT THEY'RE DOING. I EXPECT THEY'LL INTRODUCE A MILD SEDATION GAS TO KEEP THEM QUIET WHILE THEY GET US OUT.
MEANWHILE, ON TRACY ISLAND...
ALL SET, MR. TRACY!
F.A.B., BRAINS. THUNDERBIRD 2 IMMEDIATE LAUNCH!
A SPEAKER BOOMS IN THE GIANT MACHINE'S BAY...
THUNDERBIRD 2 IS GO! REPEAT... THUNDERBIRD 2 IS GO!
CURSES! I NEED MORE TIME TO COMPLETE MY PHOTOGRAPHY...
BUT IF THUNDERBIRD 2 DOESN'T TAKE OFF, TRACY WILL INVESTIGATE! MY GAME WILL BE UP...

Artist: Frank Bellamy

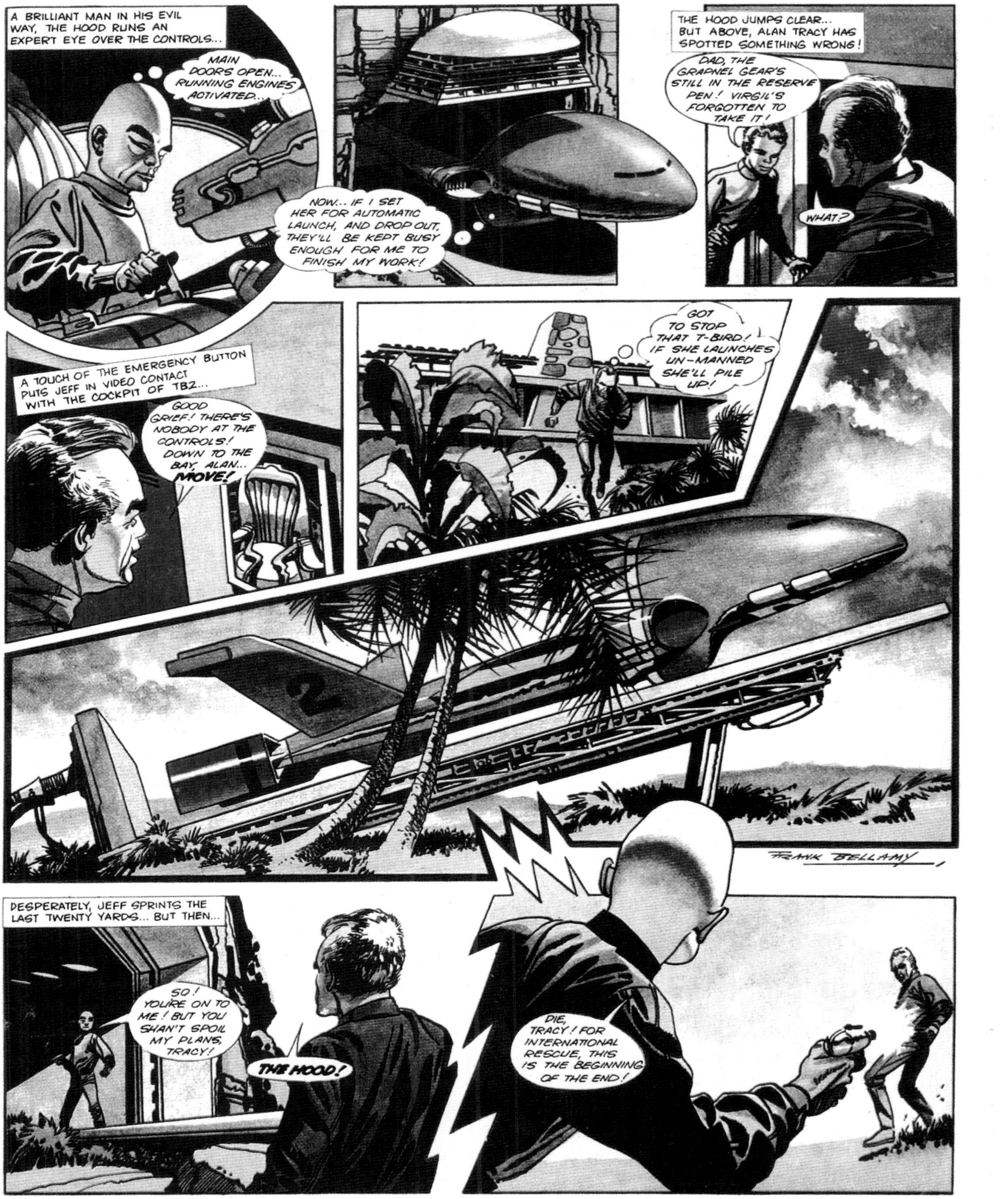
A BRILLIANT MAN IN HIS EVIL WAY, THE HOOD RUNS AN EXPERT EYE OVER THE CONTROLS...
MAIN DOORS OPEN... RUNNING ENGINES ACTIVATED...
NOW... IF I SET HER FOR AUTOMATIC LAUNCH, AND DROP OUT, THEY'LL BE KEPT BUSY ENOUGH FOR ME TO FINISH MY WORK!
THE HOOD JUMPS CLEAR... BUT ABOVE, ALAN TRACY HAS SPOTTED SOMETHING WRONG!
DAD, THE GRAPNEL GEAR'S STILL IN THE RESERVE PEN! VIRGIL'S FORGOTTEN TO TAKE IT!
WHAT?
A TOUCH OF THE EMERGENCY BUTTON PUTS JEFF IN VIDEO CONTACT WITH THE COCKPIT OF TB2...
GOOD GRIEF! THERE'S NOBODY AT THE CONTROLS! DOWN TO THE BAY, ALAN... MOVE!
GOT TO STOP THAT T-BIRD! IF SHE LAUNCHES UN-MANNED SHE'LL PILE UP!
FRANK BELLAMY
DESPERATELY, JEFF SPRINTS THE LAST TWENTY YARDS... BUT THEN...
SO! YOU'RE ON TO ME! BUT YOU SHAN'T SPOIL MY PLANS, TRACY!
THE HOOD!
DIE, TRACY! FOR INTERNATIONAL RESCUE, THIS IS THE BEGINNING OF THE END!

THUNDERBIRDS

Part 7 - dateline 01 March 2069

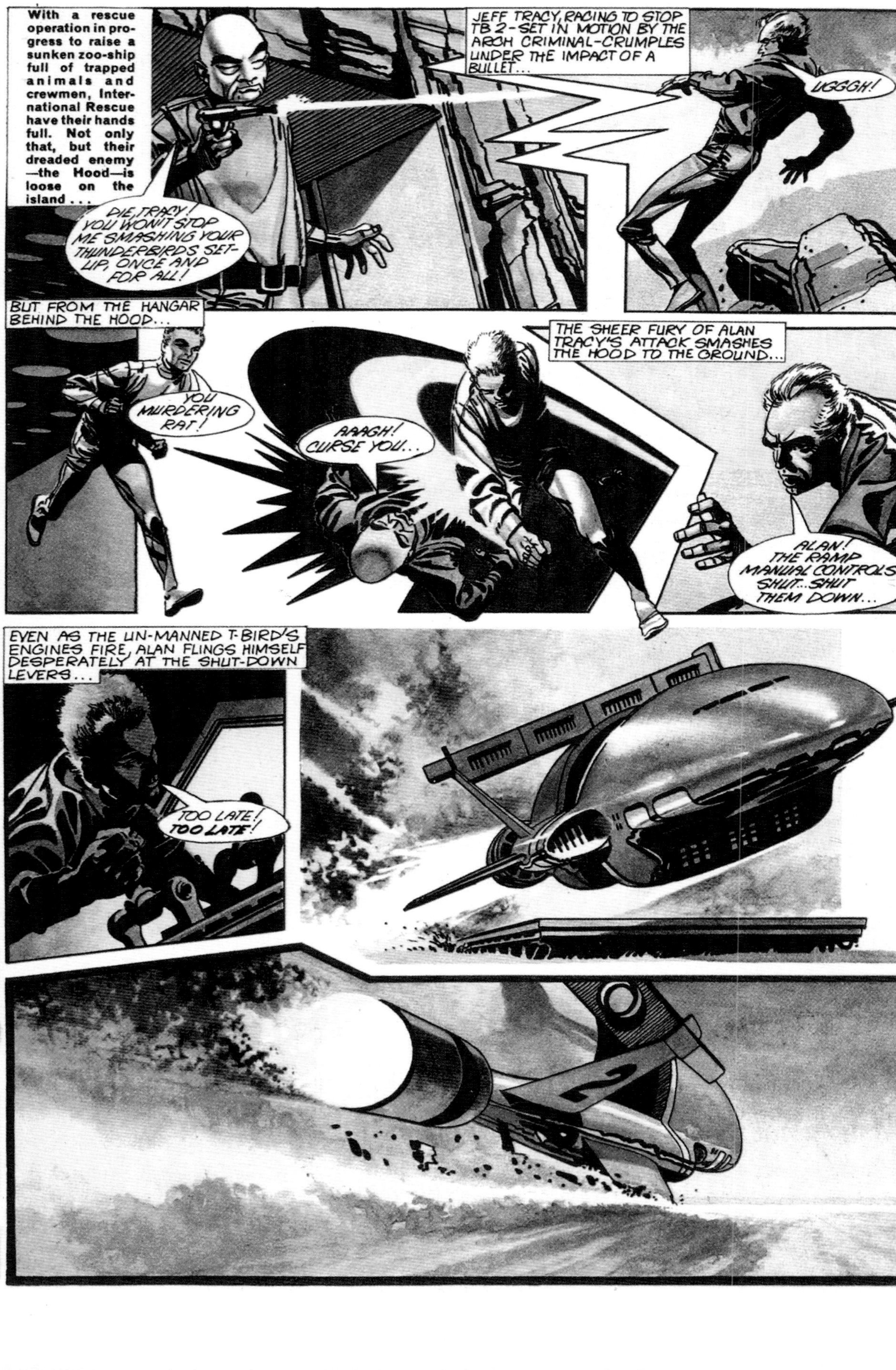
With a rescue operation in progress to raise a sunken zoo-ship full of trapped animals and crewmen, International Rescue have their hands full. Not only that, but their dreaded enemy —the Hood—is loose on the island . . .
DIE, TRACY! YOU WON'T STOP ME SMASHING YOUR THUNDERBIRDS SET-UP, ONCE AND FOR ALL!
JEFF TRACY, RACING TO STOP TB 2-SET IN MOTION BY THE ARCH CRIMINAL-CRUMPLES UNDER THE IMPACT OF A BULLET...
UGGGH!
BUT FROM THE HANGAR BEHIND THE HOOD...
YOU MURDERING RAT!
THE SHEER FURY OF ALAN TRACY'S ATTACK SMASHES THE HOOD TO THE GROUND...
AAAGH! CURSE YOU...
ALAN! THE RAMP MANUAL CONTROLS... SHUT... SHUT THEM DOWN...
EVEN AS THE UN-MANNED T-BIRD'S ENGINES FIRE, ALAN FLINGS HIMSELF DESPERATELY AT THE SHUT-DOWN LEVERS...
TOO LATE! TOO LATE!
2

Artist: Frank Bellamy

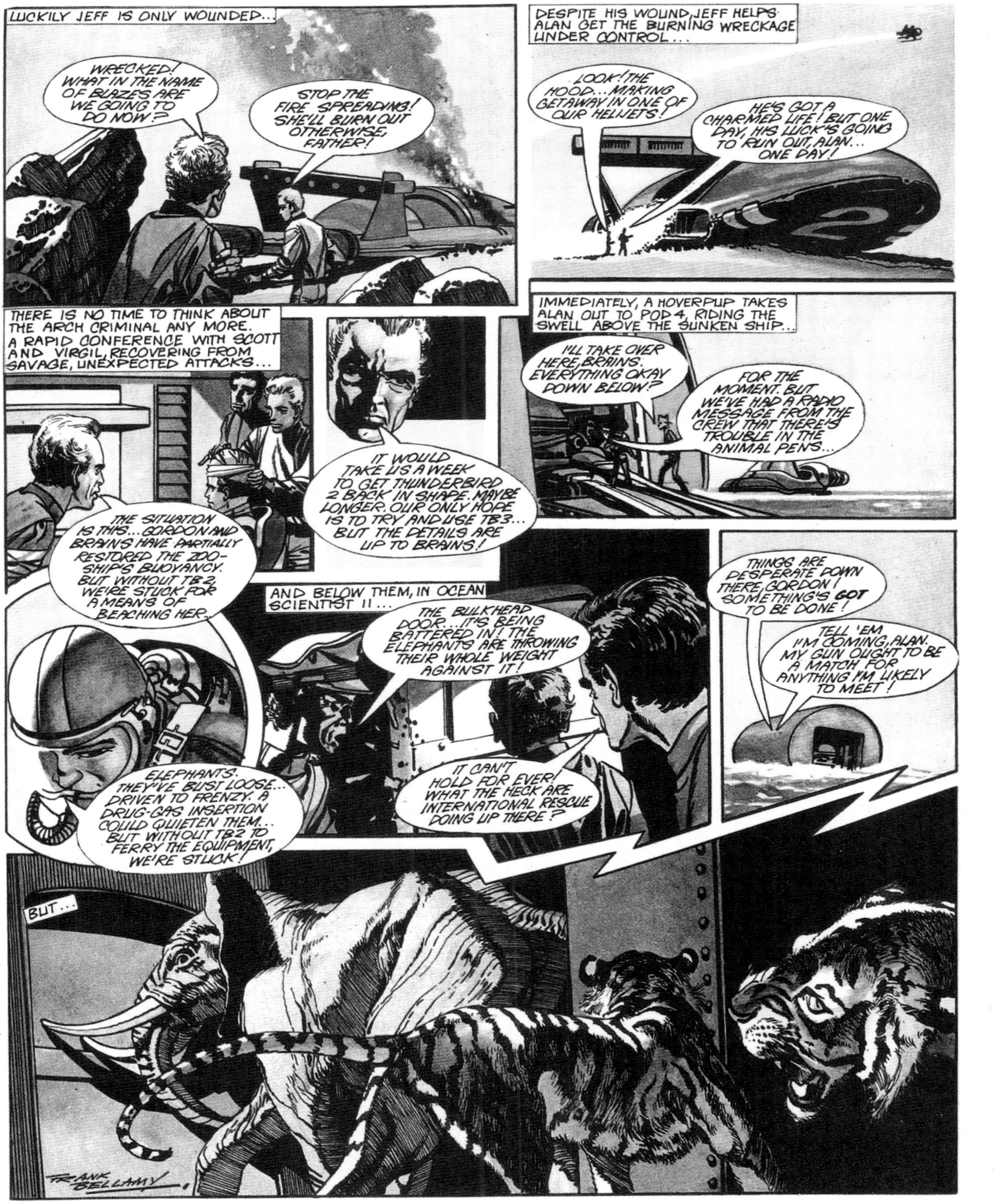
LUCKILY JEFF IS ONLY WOUNDED...
WRECKED! WHAT IN THE NAME OF BLAZES ARE WE GOING TO DO NOW?
STOP THE FIRE SPREADING! SHE'LL BURN OUT OTHERWISE, FATHER!
DESPITE HIS WOUND, JEFF HELPS ALAN GET THE BURNING WRECKAGE UNDER CONTROL...
LOOK! THE HOOD... MAKING GETAWAY IN ONE OF OUR HELIJETS!
HE'S GOT A CHARMED LIFE! BUT ONE DAY, HIS LUCK'S GOING TO RUN OUT, ALAN... ONE DAY!
THERE IS NO TIME TO THINK ABOUT THE ARCH CRIMINAL ANY MORE. A RAPID CONFERENCE WITH SCOTT AND VIRGIL, RECOVERING FROM SAVAGE, UNEXPECTED ATTACKS...
IT WOULD TAKE US A WEEK TO GET THUNDERBIRD 2 BACK IN SHAPE. MAYBE LONGER. OUR ONLY HOPE IS TO TRY AND USE TB3... BUT THE DETAILS ARE UP TO BRAINS!
THE SITUATION IS THIS... GORDON AND BRAINS HAVE PARTIALLY RESTORED THE ZOO-SHIP'S BUOYANCY. BUT WITHOUT TB2, WE'RE STUCK FOR A MEANS OF BEACHING HER...
IMMEDIATELY, A HOVERPUP TAKES ALAN OUT TO POD 4, RIDING THE SWELL ABOVE THE SUNKEN SHIP...
I'LL TAKE OVER HERE, BRAINS. EVERYTHING OKAY DOWN BELOW?
FOR THE MOMENT. BUT WE'VE HAD A RADIO MESSAGE FROM THE CREW THAT THERE'S TROUBLE IN THE ANIMAL PENS...
AND BELOW THEM, IN OCEAN SCIENTIST II...
THE BULKHEAD DOOR... IT'S BEING BATTERED IN! THE ELEPHANTS ARE THROWING THEIR WHOLE WEIGHT AGAINST IT!
IT CAN'T HOLD FOR EVER! WHAT THE HECK ARE INTERNATIONAL RESCUE DOING UP THERE?
ELEPHANTS. THEY'VE BUST LOOSE... DRIVEN TO FRENZY. A DRUG-GAS INSERTION COULD QUIETEN THEM... BUT WITHOUT TB2 TO FERRY THE EQUIPMENT, WE'RE STUCK!
THINGS ARE DESPERATE DOWN THERE, GORDON! SOMETHING'S GOT TO BE DONE!
TELL 'EM I'M COMING, ALAN. MY GUN OUGHT TO BE A MATCH FOR ANYTHING I'M LIKELY TO MEET!
BUT...
FRANK BELLAMY

THUNDERBIRDS

Part 8 - dateline 08 March 2069

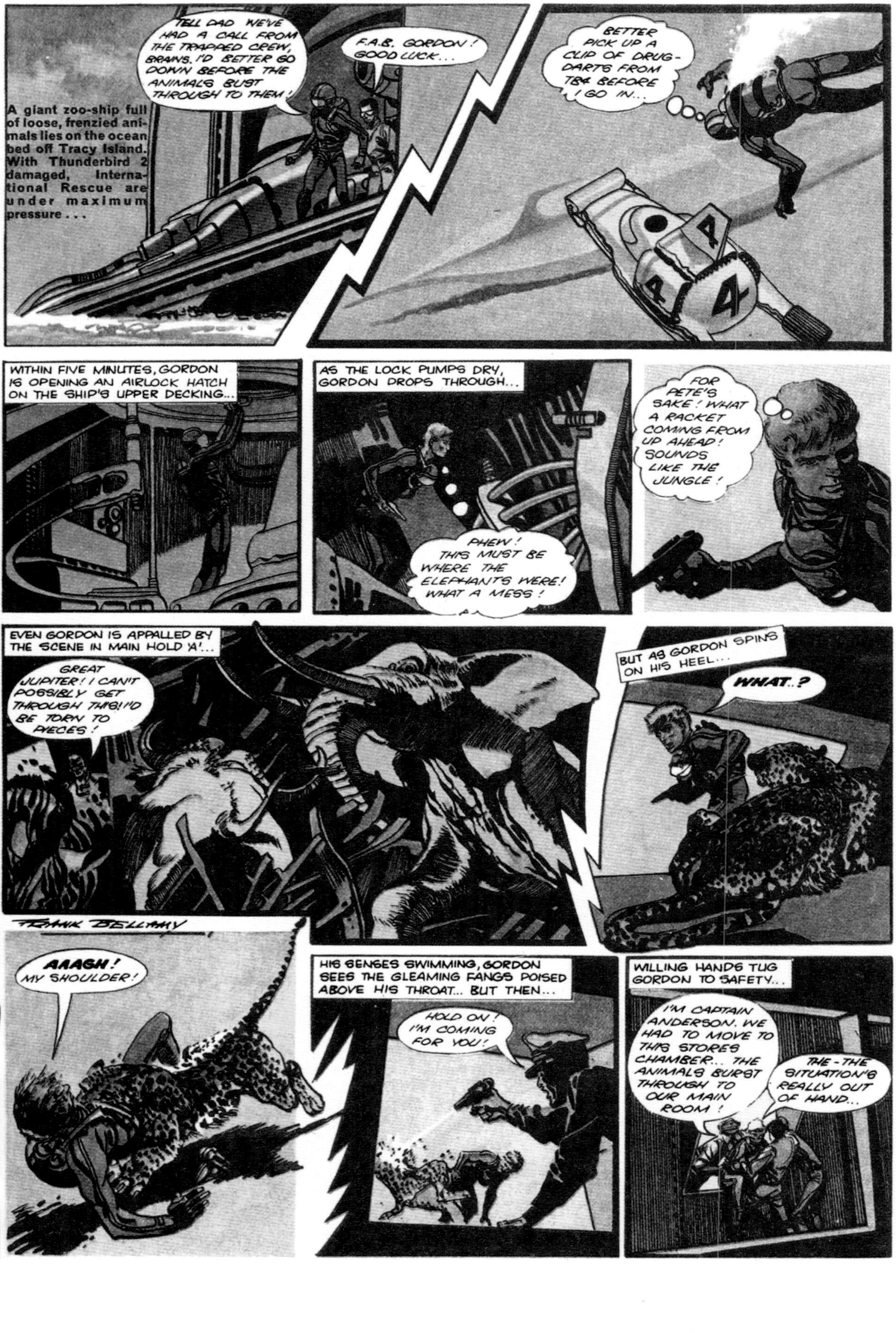
A giant zoo-ship full of loose, frenzied animals lies on the ocean bed off Tracy Island. With Thunderbird 2 damaged, International Rescue are under maximum pressure . . .
TELL DAD WE'VE HAD A CALL FROM THE TRAPPED CREW, BRAINS. I'D BETTER GO DOWN BEFORE THE ANIMALS BUST THROUGH TO THEM!
F.A.B. GORDON! GOOD LUCK...
BETTER PICK UP A CLIP OF DRUG-DARTS FROM TB4 BEFORE I GO IN...
4
WITHIN FIVE MINUTES, GORDON IS OPENING AN AIRLOCK HATCH ON THE SHIP'S UPPER DECKING...
AS THE LOCK PUMPS DRY, GORDON DROPS THROUGH...
PHEW! THIS MUST BE WHERE THE ELEPHANTS WERE! WHAT A MESS!
FOR PETE'S SAKE! WHAT A RACKET COMING FROM UP AHEAD! SOUNDS LIKE THE JUNGLE!
EVEN GORDON IS APPALLED BY THE SCENE IN MAIN HOLD 'A'...
GREAT JUPITER! I CAN'T POSSIBLY GET THROUGH THIS! I'D BE TORN TO PIECES!
BUT AS GORDON SPINS ON HIS HEEL...
WHAT..?
FRANK BELLAMY
AAAGH! MY SHOULDER!
HIS SENSES SWIMMING, GORDON SEES THE GLEAMING FANGS POISED ABOVE HIS THROAT... BUT THEN...
HOLD ON! I'M COMING FOR YOU!
WILLING HANDS TUG GORDON TO SAFETY...
I'M CAPTAIN ANDERSON. WE HAD TO MOVE TO THIS STORES CHAMBER... THE ANIMALS BURST THROUGH TO OUR MAIN ROOM!
THE-THE SITUATION'S REALLY OUT OF HAND...

Artist: Frank Bellamy

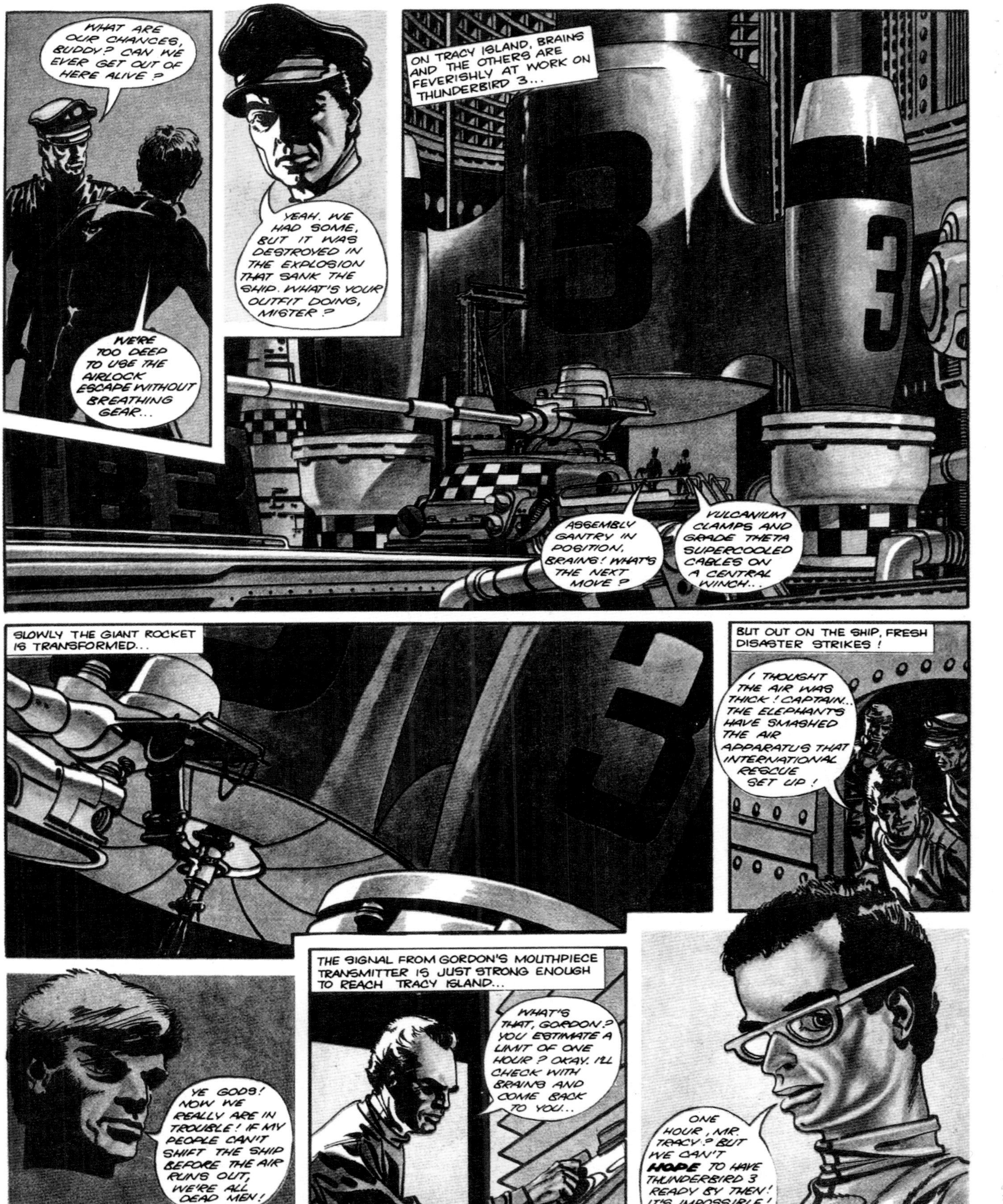
WHAT ARE OUR CHANCES, BUDDY? CAN WE EVER GET OUT OF HERE ALIVE?
WE'RE TOO DEEP TO USE THE AIRLOCK ESCAPE WITHOUT BREATHING GEAR...
YEAH. WE HAD SOME, BUT IT WAS DESTROYED IN THE EXPLOSION THAT SANK THE SHIP. WHAT'S YOUR OUTFIT DOING, MISTER?
ON TRACY ISLAND, BRAINS AND THE OTHERS ARE FEVERISHLY AT WORK ON THUNDERBIRD 3...
ASSEMBLY GANTRY IN POSITION, BRAINS! WHAT'S THE NEXT MOVE?
VULCANIUM CLAMPS AND GRADE THETA SUPERCOOLED CABLES ON A CENTRAL WINCH...
SLOWLY THE GIANT ROCKET IS TRANSFORMED...
BUT OUT ON THE SHIP, FRESH DISASTER STRIKES!
I THOUGHT THE AIR WAS THICK! CAPTAIN... THE ELEPHANTS HAVE SMASHED THE AIR APPARATUS THAT INTERNATIONAL RESCUE SET UP!
YE GODS! NOW WE REALLY ARE IN TROUBLE! IF MY PEOPLE CAN'T SHIFT THE SHIP BEFORE THE AIR RUNS OUT, WE'RE ALL DEAD MEN!
THE SIGNAL FROM GORDON'S MOUTHPIECE TRANSMITTER IS JUST STRONG ENOUGH TO REACH TRACY ISLAND...
WHAT'S THAT, GORDON? YOU ESTIMATE A LIMIT OF ONE HOUR? OKAY. I'LL CHECK WITH BRAINS AND COME BACK TO YOU...
ONE HOUR, MR. TRACY? BUT WE CAN'T HOPE TO HAVE THUNDERBIRD 3 READY BY THEN! IT'S IMPOSSIBLE!

Part 9 - dateline 15 March 2069

THUNDERBIRDS

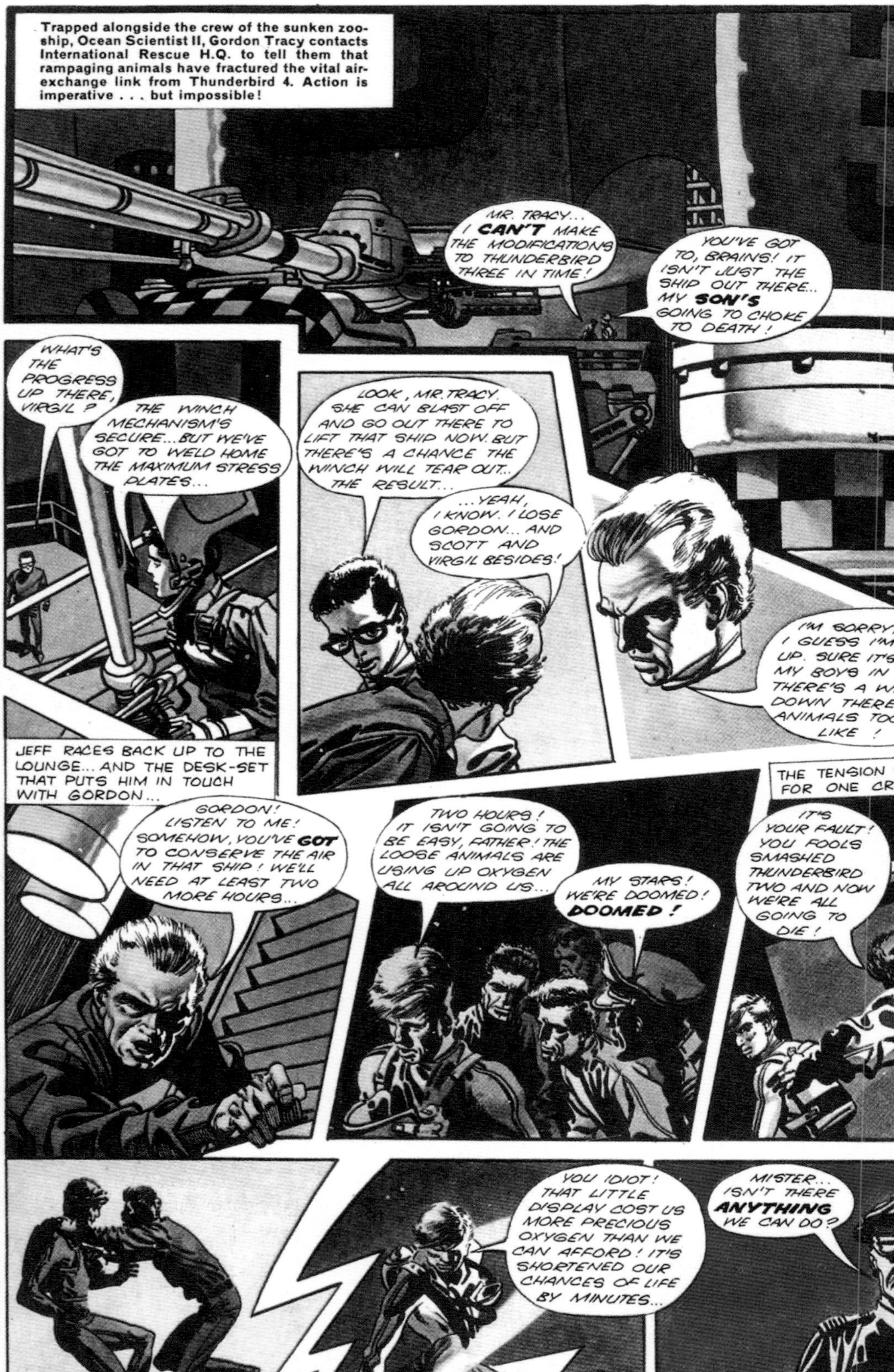
Trapped alongside the crew of the sunken zoo-ship, Ocean Scientist II, Gordon Tracy contacts International Rescue H.Q. to tell them that rampaging animals have fractured the vital air-exchange link from Thunderbird 4. Action is imperative . . . but impossible!
MR. TRACY... I CAN'T MAKE THE MODIFICATIONS TO THUNDERBIRD THREE IN TIME!
YOU'VE GOT TO, BRAINS! IT ISN'T JUST THE SHIP OUT THERE... MY SON'S GOING TO CHOKE TO DEATH!
WHAT'S THE PROGRESS UP THERE, VIRGIL?
THE WINCH MECHANISM'S SECURE... BUT WE'VE GOT TO WELD HOME THE MAXIMUM STRESS PLATES...
LOOK, MR. TRACY. SHE CAN BLAST OFF AND GO OUT THERE TO LIFT THAT SHIP NOW. BUT THERE'S A CHANCE THE WINCH WILL TEAR OUT... THE RESULT...
...YEAH, I KNOW. I LOSE GORDON... AND SCOTT AND VIRGIL BESIDES!
I'M SORRY, BRAINS. I GUESS I'M TOO HET UP. SURE IT'S NOT JUST MY BOYS IN DANGER. THERE'S A WHOLE CREW DOWN THERE... AND THE ANIMALS TOO, IF YOU LIKE!
JEFF RACES BACK UP TO THE LOUNGE... AND THE DESK-SET THAT PUTS HIM IN TOUCH WITH GORDON...
GORDON! LISTEN TO ME! SOMEHOW, YOU'VE GOT TO CONSERVE THE AIR IN THAT SHIP! WE'LL NEED AT LEAST TWO MORE HOURS...
TWO HOURS! IT ISN'T GOING TO BE EASY, FATHER! THE LOOSE ANIMALS ARE USING UP OXYGEN ALL AROUND US...
MY STARS! WE'RE DOOMED! DOOMED!
THE TENSION IS TOO MUCH FOR ONE CREWMAN...
IT'S YOUR FAULT! YOU FOOLS SMASHED THUNDERBIRD TWO AND NOW WE'RE ALL GOING TO DIE!
YOU IDIOT! THAT LITTLE DISPLAY COST US MORE PRECIOUS OXYGEN THAN WE CAN AFFORD! IT'S SHORTENED OUR CHANCES OF LIFE BY MINUTES...
MISTER... ISN'T THERE ANYTHING WE CAN DO?
NOTHING! EXCEPT SIT STILL, KEEP QUIET... AND HOPE!

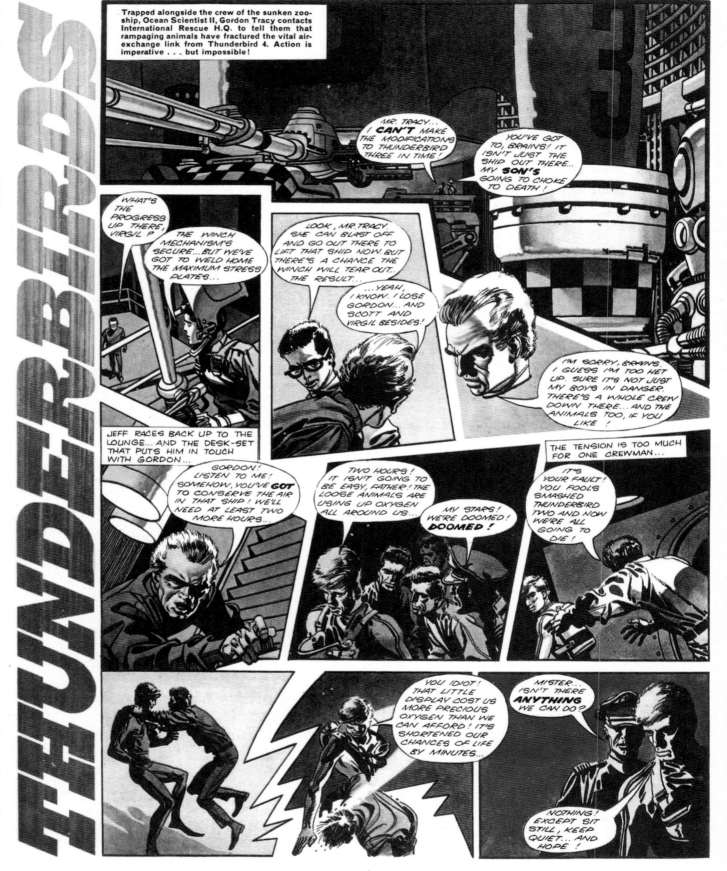

Artist: Frank Bellamy

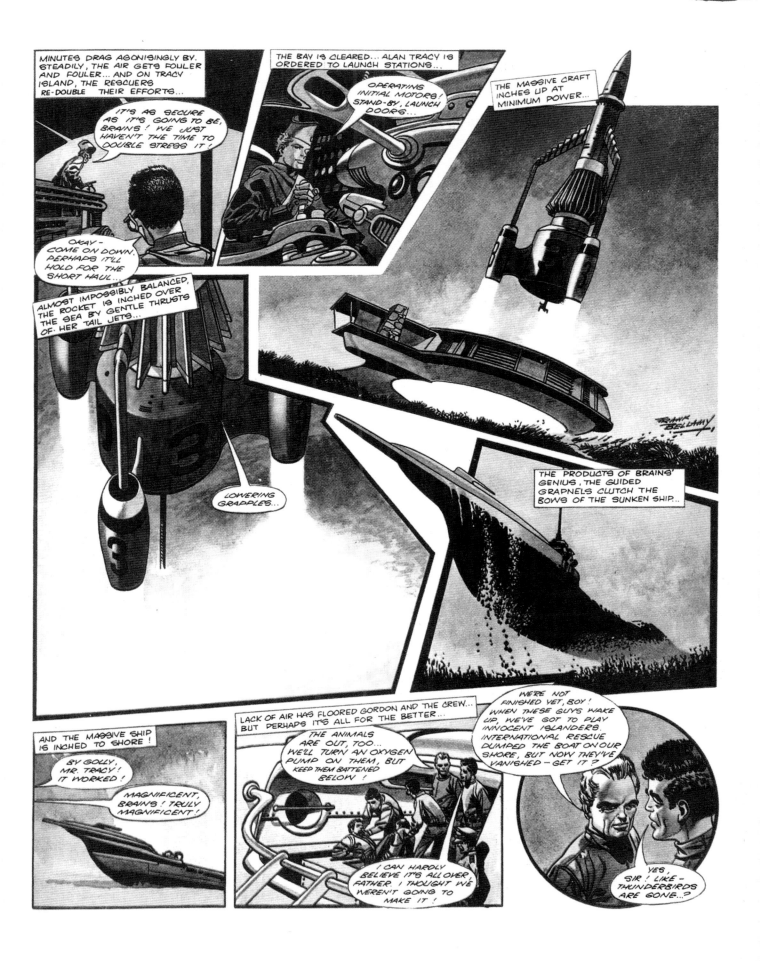

MINUTES DRAG AGONISINGLY BY. STEADILY, THE AIR GETS FOULER AND FOULER... AND ON TRACY ISLAND, THE RESCUERS RE-DOUBLE THEIR EFFORTS...

IT'S AS SECURE AS IT'S GOING TO BE, BRAINS! WE JUST HAVEN'T THE TIME TO DOUBLE STRESS IT!

OKAY — COME ON DOWN. PERHAPS IT'LL HOLD FOR THE SHORT HAUL...

THE BAY IS CLEARED... ALAN TRACY IS ORDERED TO LAUNCH STATIONS...

OPERATING INITIAL MOTORS! STAND-BY, LAUNCH DOORS...

THE MASSIVE CRAFT INCHES UP AT MINIMUM POWER...

ALMOST IMPOSSIBLY BALANCED, THE ROCKET IS INCHED OVER THE SEA BY GENTLE THRUSTS OF HER TAIL JETS...

LOWERING GRAPPLES...

THE PRODUCTS OF BRAINS' GENIUS, THE GUIDED GRAPNELS CLUTCH THE BOWS OF THE SUNKEN SHIP...

AND THE MASSIVE SHIP IS INCHED TO SHORE!

BY GOLLY, MR. TRACY! IT WORKED!

MAGNIFICENT, BRAINS! TRULY MAGNIFICENT!

LACK OF AIR HAS FLOORED GORDON AND THE CREW... BUT PERHAPS IT'S ALL FOR THE BETTER...

THE ANIMALS ARE OUT, TOO... WE'LL TURN AN OXYGEN PUMP ON THEM, BUT KEEP THEM BATTENED BELOW!

I CAN HARDLY BELIEVE IT'S ALL OVER, FATHER. I THOUGHT WE WEREN'T GOING TO MAKE IT!

WE'RE NOT FINISHED YET, BOY! WHEN THESE GUYS WAKE UP, WE'VE GOT TO PLAY INNOCENT ISLANDERS. INTERNATIONAL RESCUE DUMPED THE BOAT ON OUR SHORE, BUT NOW THEY'VE VANISHED — GET IT?

YES, SIR! LIKE — THUNDERBIRDS ARE GONE...?

Part 1 - dateline 24 May 2069

THUNDERBIRDS

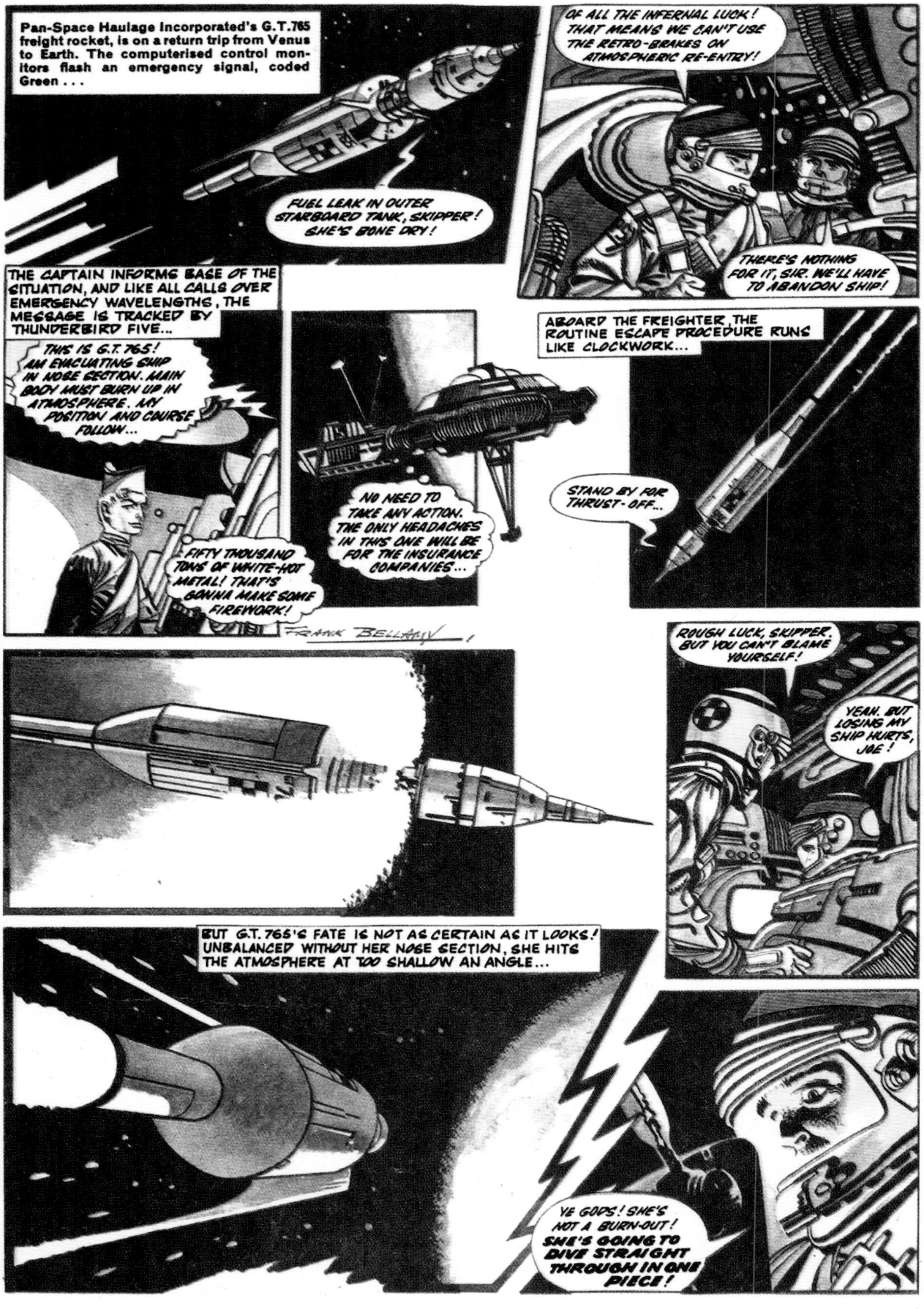
Pan-Space Haulage Incorporated's G.T.765 freight rocket, is on a return trip from Venus to Earth. The computerised control monitors flash an emergency signal, coded Green . . .
FUEL LEAK IN OUTER STARBOARD TANK, SKIPPER! SHE'S BONE DRY!
OF ALL THE INFERNAL LUCK! THAT MEANS WE CAN'T USE THE RETRO-BRAKES ON ATMOSPHERIC RE-ENTRY!
THERE'S NOTHING FOR IT, SIR. WE'LL HAVE TO ABANDON SHIP!
THE CAPTAIN INFORMS BASE OF THE SITUATION, AND LIKE ALL CALLS OVER EMERGENCY WAVELENGTHS, THE MESSAGE IS TRACKED BY THUNDERBIRD FIVE...
THIS IS G.T. 765! AM EVACUATING SHIP IN NOSE SECTION. MAIN BODY MUST BURN UP IN ATMOSPHERE. MY POSITION AND COURSE FOLLOW...
FIFTY THOUSAND TONS OF WHITE-HOT METAL! THAT'S GONNA MAKE SOME FIREWORK!
NO NEED TO TAKE ANY ACTION. THE ONLY HEADACHES IN THIS ONE WILL BE FOR THE INSURANCE COMPANIES...
FRANK BELLAMY
ABOARD THE FREIGHTER, THE ROUTINE ESCAPE PROCEDURE RUNS LIKE CLOCKWORK...
STAND BY FOR THRUST-OFF...
ROUGH LUCK, SKIPPER. BUT YOU CAN'T BLAME YOURSELF!
YEAH. BUT LOSING MY SHIP HURTS, JOE!
BUT G.T. 765'S FATE IS NOT AS CERTAIN AS IT LOOKS! UNBALANCED WITHOUT HER NOSE SECTION, SHE HITS THE ATMOSPHERE AT TOO SHALLOW AN ANGLE...
YE GODS! SHE'S NOT A BURN-OUT! SHE'S GOING TO DIVE STRAIGHT THROUGH IN ONE PIECE!

Artist: Frank Bellamy

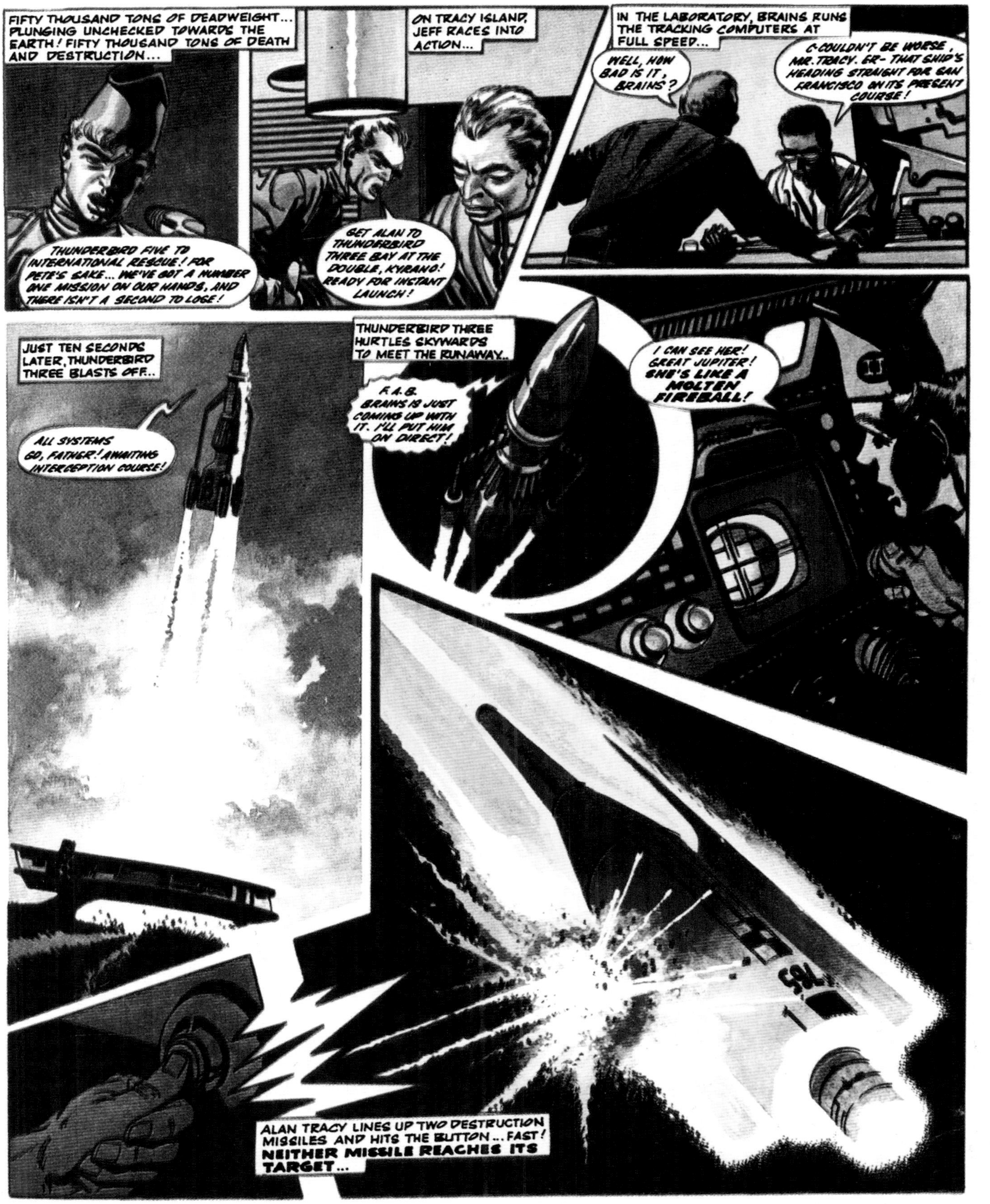
FIFTY THOUSAND TONS OF DEADWEIGHT... PLUNGING UNCHECKED TOWARDS THE EARTH! FIFTY THOUSAND TONS OF DEATH AND DESTRUCTION...
THUNDERBIRD FIVE TO INTERNATIONAL RESCUE! FOR PETE'S SAKE... WE'VE GOT A NUMBER ONE MISSION ON OUR HANDS, AND THERE ISN'T A SECOND TO LOSE!
ON TRACY ISLAND, JEFF RACES INTO ACTION...
GET ALAN TO THUNDERBIRD THREE BAY AT THE DOUBLE, KYRANO! READY FOR INSTANT LAUNCH!
IN THE LABORATORY, BRAINS RUNS THE TRACKING COMPUTERS AT FULL SPEED...
WELL, HOW BAD IS IT, BRAINS?
C-COULDN'T BE WORSE, MR. TRACY. ER- THAT SHIP'S HEADING STRAIGHT FOR SAN FRANCISCO ON ITS PRESENT COURSE!
JUST TEN SECONDS LATER, THUNDERBIRD THREE BLASTS OFF...
ALL SYSTEMS GO, FATHER! AWAITING INTERCEPTION COURSE!
THUNDERBIRD THREE HURTLES SKYWARDS TO MEET THE RUNAWAY...
F.A.B. BRAINS IS JUST COMING UP WITH IT. I'LL PUT HIM ON DIRECT!
I CAN SEE HER! GREAT JUPITER! SHE'S LIKE A MOLTEN FIREBALL!
ALAN TRACY LINES UP TWO DESTRUCTION MISSILES AND HITS THE BUTTON... FAST! NEITHER MISSILE REACHES ITS TARGET...

THUNDERBIRDS

Part 2 - dateline 31 May 2069

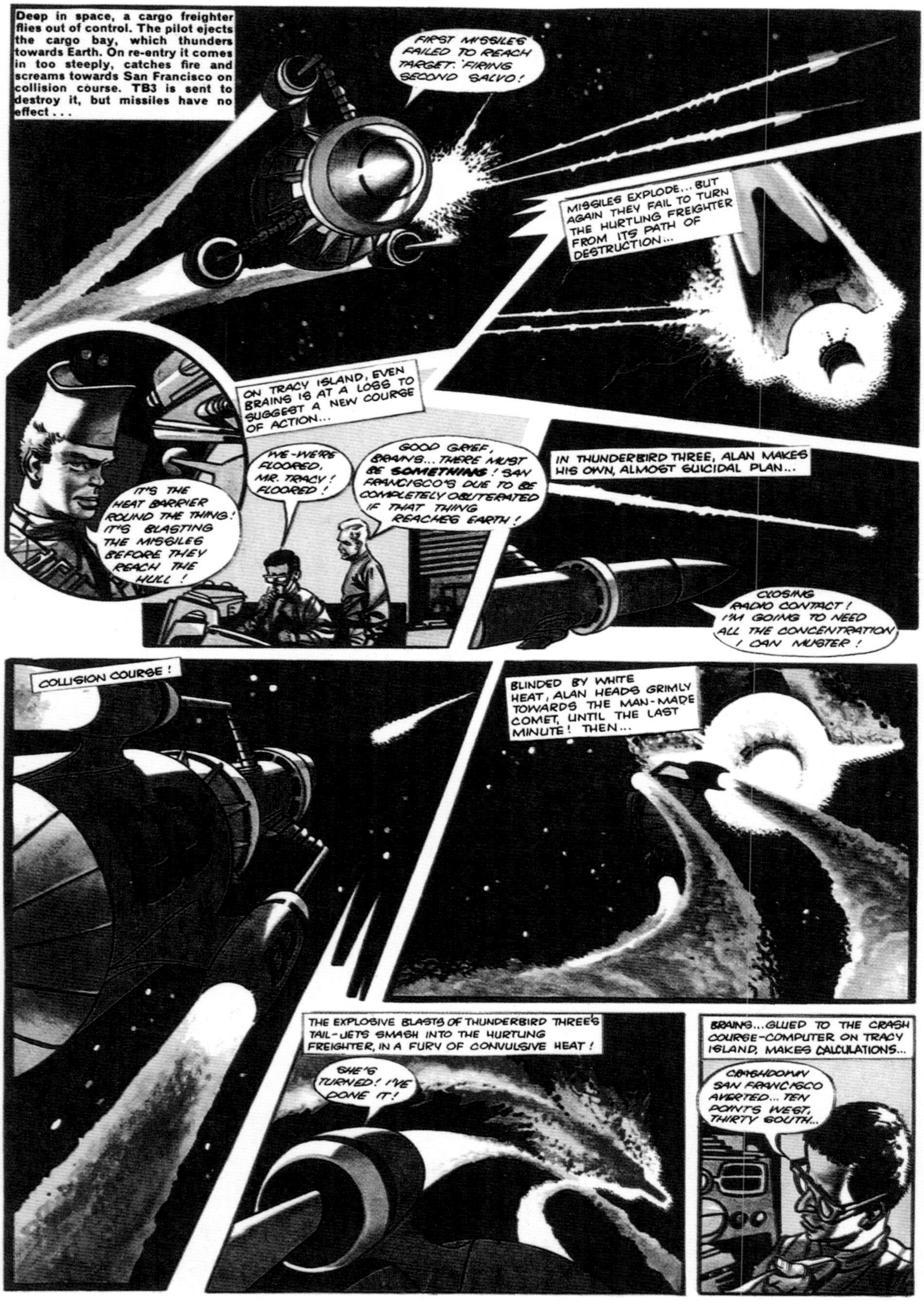
Deep in space, a cargo freighter flies out of control. The pilot ejects the cargo bay, which thunders towards Earth. On re-entry it comes in too steeply, catches fire and screams towards San Francisco on collision course. TB3 is sent to destroy it, but missiles have no effect . . .
FIRST MISSILES FAILED TO REACH TARGET. FIRING SECOND SALVO!
MISSILES EXPLODE... BUT AGAIN THEY FAIL TO TURN THE HURTLING FREIGHTER FROM ITS PATH OF DESTRUCTION...
ON TRACY ISLAND, EVEN BRAINS IS AT A LOSS TO SUGGEST A NEW COURSE OF ACTION...
IT'S THE HEAT BARRIER ROUND THE THING! IT'S BLASTING THE MISSILES BEFORE THEY REACH THE HULL!
WE-WE'RE FLOORED, MR. TRACY! FLOORED!
GOOD GRIEF, BRAINS... THERE MUST BE SOMETHING! SAN FRANCISCO'S DUE TO BE COMPLETELY OBLITERATED IF THAT THING REACHES EARTH!
IN THUNDERBIRD THREE, ALAN MAKES HIS OWN, ALMOST SUICIDAL PLAN...
CLOSING RADIO CONTACT! I'M GOING TO NEED ALL THE CONCENTRATION I CAN MUSTER!
COLLISION COURSE!
BLINDED BY WHITE HEAT, ALAN HEADS GRIMLY TOWARDS THE MAN-MADE COMET, UNTIL THE LAST MINUTE! THEN...
THE EXPLOSIVE BLASTS OF THUNDERBIRD THREE'S TAIL-JETS SMASH INTO THE HURTLING FREIGHTER, IN A FURY OF CONVULSIVE HEAT!
SHE'S TURNED! I'VE DONE IT!
BRAINS... GLUED TO THE CRASH COURSE-COMPUTER ON TRACY ISLAND, MAKES CALCULATIONS...
CRASHDOWN SAN FRANCISCO AVERTED... TEN POINTS WEST, THIRTY SOUTH...

Artist: Frank Bellamy

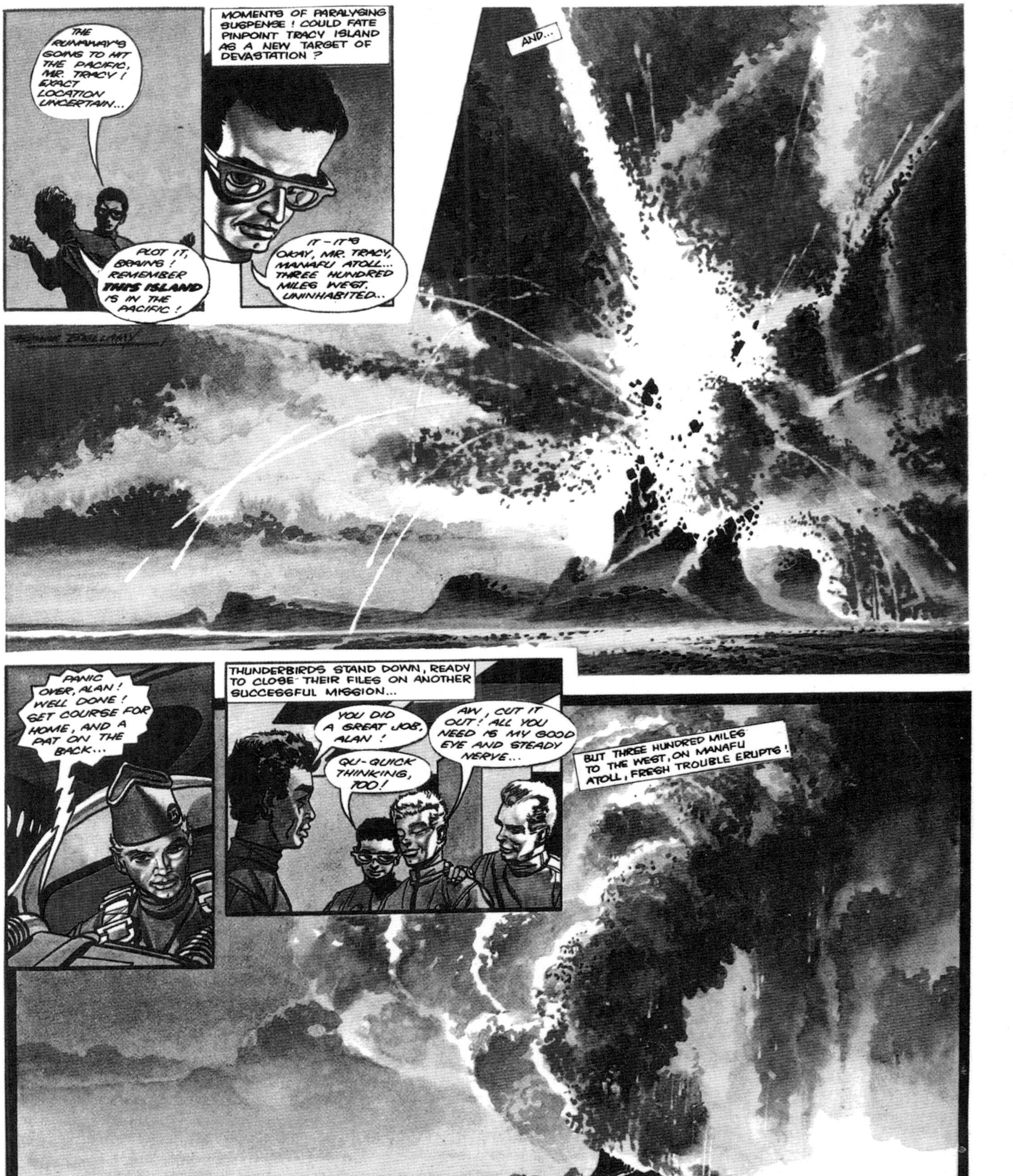
THE RUNAWAY'S GOING TO HIT THE PACIFIC, MR. TRACY! EXACT LOCATION UNCERTAIN...
PLOT IT, BRAINS! REMEMBER THIS ISLAND IS IN THE PACIFIC!
MOMENTS OF PARALYSING SUSPENSE! COULD FATE PINPOINT TRACY ISLAND AS A NEW TARGET OF DEVASTATION?
IT - IT'S OKAY, MR. TRACY, MANAFU ATOLL... THREE HUNDRED MILES WEST. UNINHABITED...
AND...
PANIC OVER, ALAN! WELL DONE! SET COURSE FOR HOME, AND A PAT ON THE BACK...
THUNDERBIRDS STAND DOWN, READY TO CLOSE THEIR FILES ON ANOTHER SUCCESSFUL MISSION...
YOU DID A GREAT JOB, ALAN!
QU-QUICK THINKING, TOO!
AW, CUT IT OUT! ALL YOU NEED IS MY GOOD EYE AND STEADY NERVE...
BUT THREE HUNDRED MILES TO THE WEST, ON MANAFU ATOLL, FRESH TROUBLE ERUPTS!

Part 3 - dateline 07 June 2069

THUNDERBIRDS

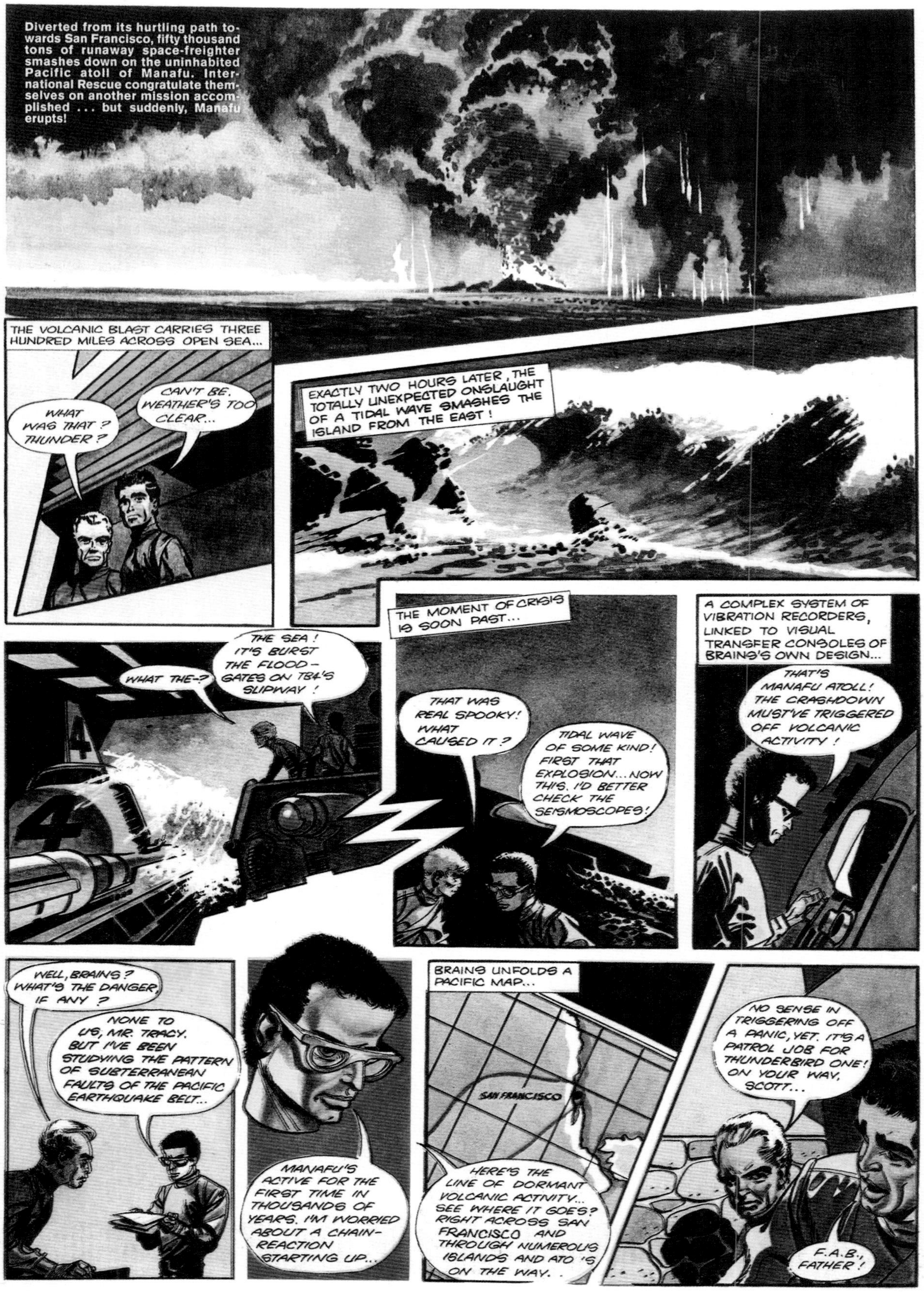
Diverted from its hurtling path towards San Francisco, fifty thousand tons of runaway space-freighter smashes down on the uninhabited Pacific atoll of Manafu. International Rescue congratulate themselves on another mission accomplished ... but suddenly, Manafu erupts!
THE VOLCANIC BLAST CARRIES THREE HUNDRED MILES ACROSS OPEN SEA...
WHAT WAS THAT? THUNDER?
CAN'T BE. WEATHER'S TOO CLEAR...
EXACTLY TWO HOURS LATER, THE TOTALLY UNEXPECTED ONSLAUGHT OF A TIDAL WAVE SMASHES THE ISLAND FROM THE EAST!
WHAT THE-?
THE SEA! IT'S BURST THE FLOOD-GATES ON TB4'S SLIPWAY!
THE MOMENT OF CRISIS IS SOON PAST...
THAT WAS REAL SPOOKY! WHAT CAUSED IT?
TIDAL WAVE OF SOME KIND! FIRST THAT EXPLOSION... NOW THIS. I'D BETTER CHECK THE SEISMOSCOPES!
A COMPLEX SYSTEM OF VIBRATION RECORDERS, LINKED TO VISUAL TRANSFER CONSOLES OF BRAINS'S OWN DESIGN...
THAT'S MANAFU ATOLL! THE CRASHDOWN MUST'VE TRIGGERED OFF VOLCANIC ACTIVITY!
WELL, BRAINS? WHAT'S THE DANGER, IF ANY?
NONE TO US, MR. TRACY. BUT I'VE BEEN STUDYING THE PATTERN OF SUBTERRANEAN FAULTS OF THE PACIFIC EARTHQUAKE BELT...
MANAFU'S ACTIVE FOR THE FIRST TIME IN THOUSANDS OF YEARS. I'M WORRIED ABOUT A CHAIN-REACTION STARTING UP...
BRAINS UNFOLDS A PACIFIC MAP...
SAN FRANCISCO
HERE'S THE LINE OF DORMANT VOLCANIC ACTIVITY... SEE WHERE IT GOES? RIGHT ACROSS SAN FRANCISCO AND THROUGH NUMEROUS ISLANDS AND ATO'S ON THE WAY...
NO SENSE IN TRIGGERING OFF A PANIC, YET. IT'S A PATROL JOB FOR THUNDERBIRD ONE! ON YOUR WAY, SCOTT...
F.A.B., FATHER!

Artist: Frank Bellamy

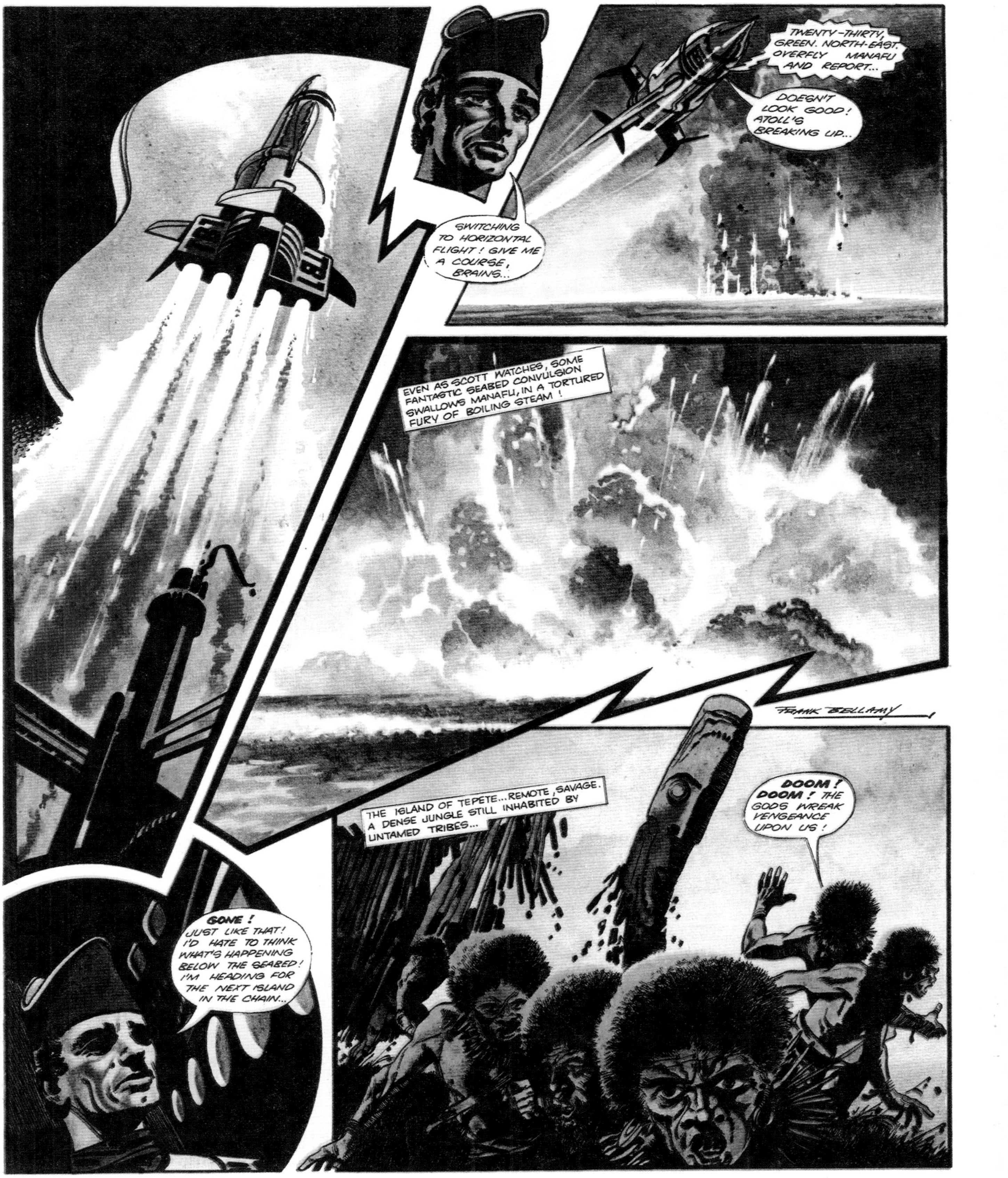
SWITCHING TO HORIZONTAL FLIGHT! GIVE ME A COURSE, BRAINS...
TWENTY-THIRTY, GREEN. NORTH-EAST. OVERFLY MANAFU AND REPORT...
DOESN'T LOOK GOOD! ATOLL'S BREAKING UP...
EVEN AS SCOTT WATCHES, SOME FANTASTIC SEABED CONVULSION SWALLOWS MANAFU, IN A TORTURED FURY OF BOILING STEAM!
FRANK BELLAMY
GONE! JUST LIKE THAT! I'D HATE TO THINK WHAT'S HAPPENING BELOW THE SEABED! I'M HEADING FOR THE NEXT ISLAND IN THE CHAIN...
THE ISLAND OF TEPETE... REMOTE, SAVAGE. A DENSE JUNGLE STILL INHABITED BY UNTAMED TRIBES...
DOOM! DOOM! THE GODS WREAK VENGEANCE UPON US!

Part 4 - dateline 14 June 2069

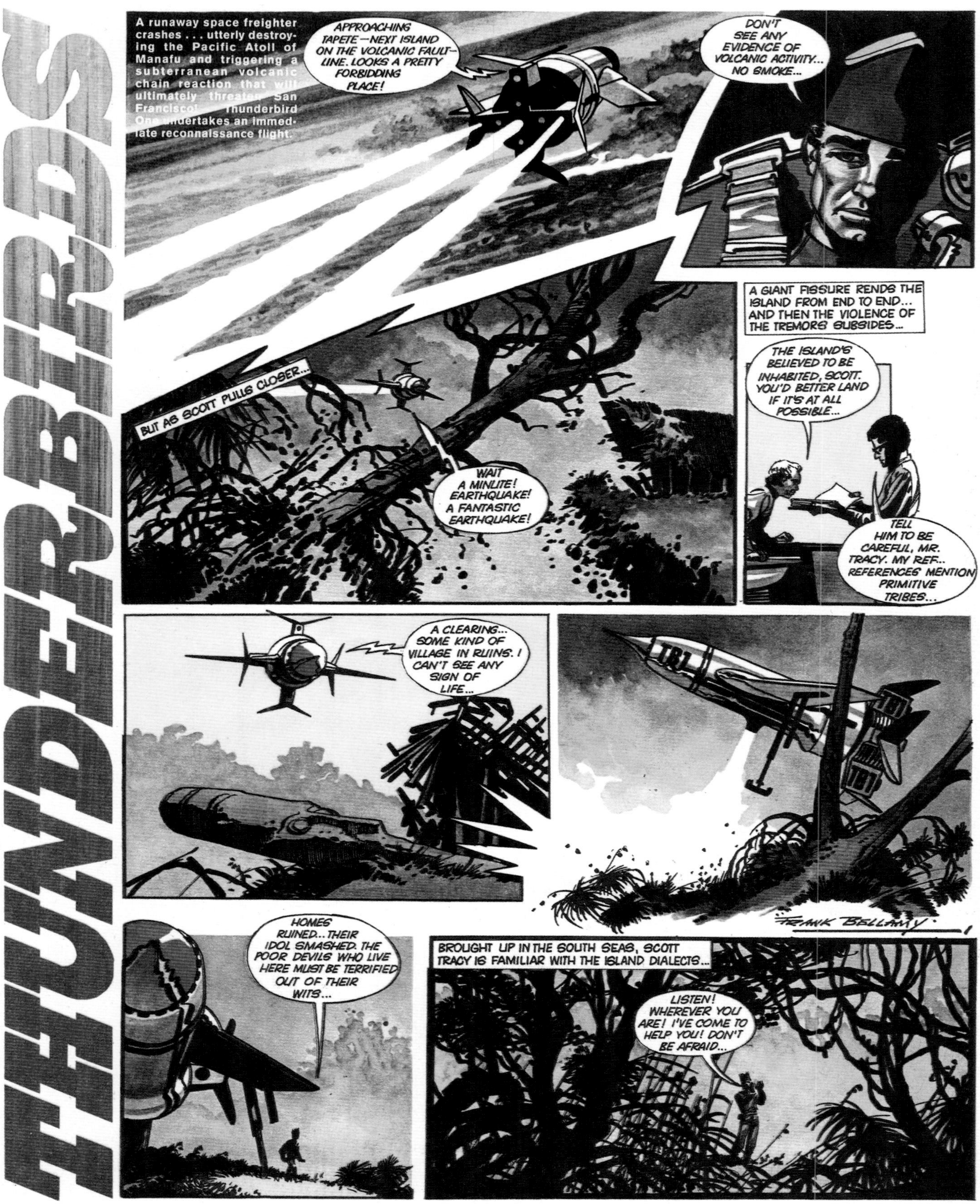
THUNDERBIRDS
A runaway space freighter crashes . . . utterly destroying the Pacific Atoll of Manafu and triggering a subterranean volcanic chain reaction that will ultimately threaten San Francisco! Thunderbird One undertakes an immediate reconnaissance flight.
APPROACHING TAPETE—NEXT ISLAND ON THE VOLCANIC FAULT-LINE. LOOKS A PRETTY FORBIDDING PLACE!
DON'T SEE ANY EVIDENCE OF VOLCANIC ACTIVITY... NO SMOKE...
BUT AS SCOTT PULLS CLOSER...
WAIT A MINUTE! EARTHQUAKE! A FANTASTIC EARTHQUAKE!
A GIANT FISSURE RENDS THE ISLAND FROM END TO END... AND THEN THE VIOLENCE OF THE TREMORS SUBSIDES...
THE ISLAND'S BELIEVED TO BE INHABITED, SCOTT. YOU'D BETTER LAND IF IT'S AT ALL POSSIBLE...
TELL HIM TO BE CAREFUL, MR. TRACY. MY REF... REFERENCES MENTION PRIMITIVE TRIBES...
A CLEARING... SOME KIND OF VILLAGE IN RUINS. I CAN'T SEE ANY SIGN OF LIFE...
TB1
FRANK BELLAMY
HOMES RUINED... THEIR IDOL SMASHED. THE POOR DEVILS WHO LIVE HERE MUST BE TERRIFIED OUT OF THEIR WITS...
BROUGHT UP IN THE SOUTH SEAS, SCOTT TRACY IS FAMILIAR WITH THE ISLAND DIALECTS...
LISTEN! WHEREVER YOU ARE! I'VE COME TO HELP YOU! DON'T BE AFRAID...

Artist: Frank Bellamy

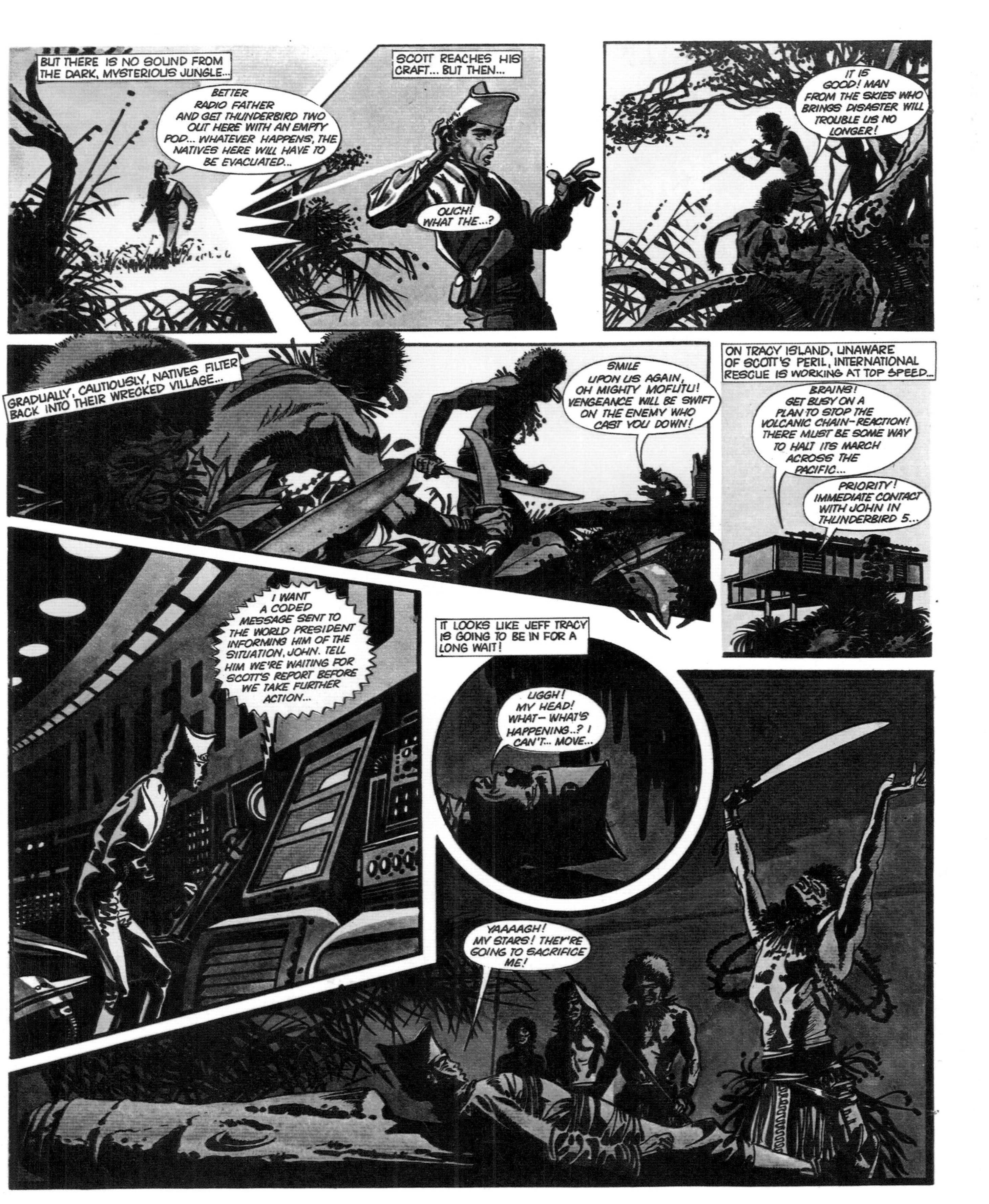
BUT THERE IS NO SOUND FROM THE DARK, MYSTERIOUS JUNGLE...
BETTER RADIO FATHER AND GET THUNDERBIRD TWO OUT HERE WITH AN EMPTY POD... WHATEVER HAPPENS, THE NATIVES HERE WILL HAVE TO BE EVACUATED...
SCOTT REACHES HIS CRAFT... BUT THEN...
OUCH! WHAT THE...?
IT IS GOOD! MAN FROM THE SKIES WHO BRINGS DISASTER WILL TROUBLE US NO LONGER!
GRADUALLY, CAUTIOUSLY, NATIVES FILTER BACK INTO THEIR WRECKED VILLAGE...
SMILE UPON US AGAIN, OH MIGHTY MOFUTU! VENGEANCE WILL BE SWIFT ON THE ENEMY WHO CAST YOU DOWN!
ON TRACY ISLAND, UNAWARE OF SCOTT'S PERIL, INTERNATIONAL RESCUE IS WORKING AT TOP SPEED...
BRAINS! GET BUSY ON A PLAN TO STOP THE VOLCANIC CHAIN-REACTION! THERE MUST BE SOME WAY TO HALT ITS MARCH ACROSS THE PACIFIC...
PRIORITY! IMMEDIATE CONTACT WITH JOHN IN THUNDERBIRD 5...
I WANT A CODED MESSAGE SENT TO THE WORLD PRESIDENT INFORMING HIM OF THE SITUATION, JOHN. TELL HIM WE'RE WAITING FOR SCOTT'S REPORT BEFORE WE TAKE FURTHER ACTION...
IT LOOKS LIKE JEFF TRACY IS GOING TO BE IN FOR A LONG WAIT!
UGGH! MY HEAD! WHAT- WHAT'S HAPPENING..? I CAN'T... MOVE...
YAAAAGH! MY STARS! THEY'RE GOING TO SACRIFICE ME!

Part 5 - dateline 21 June 2069

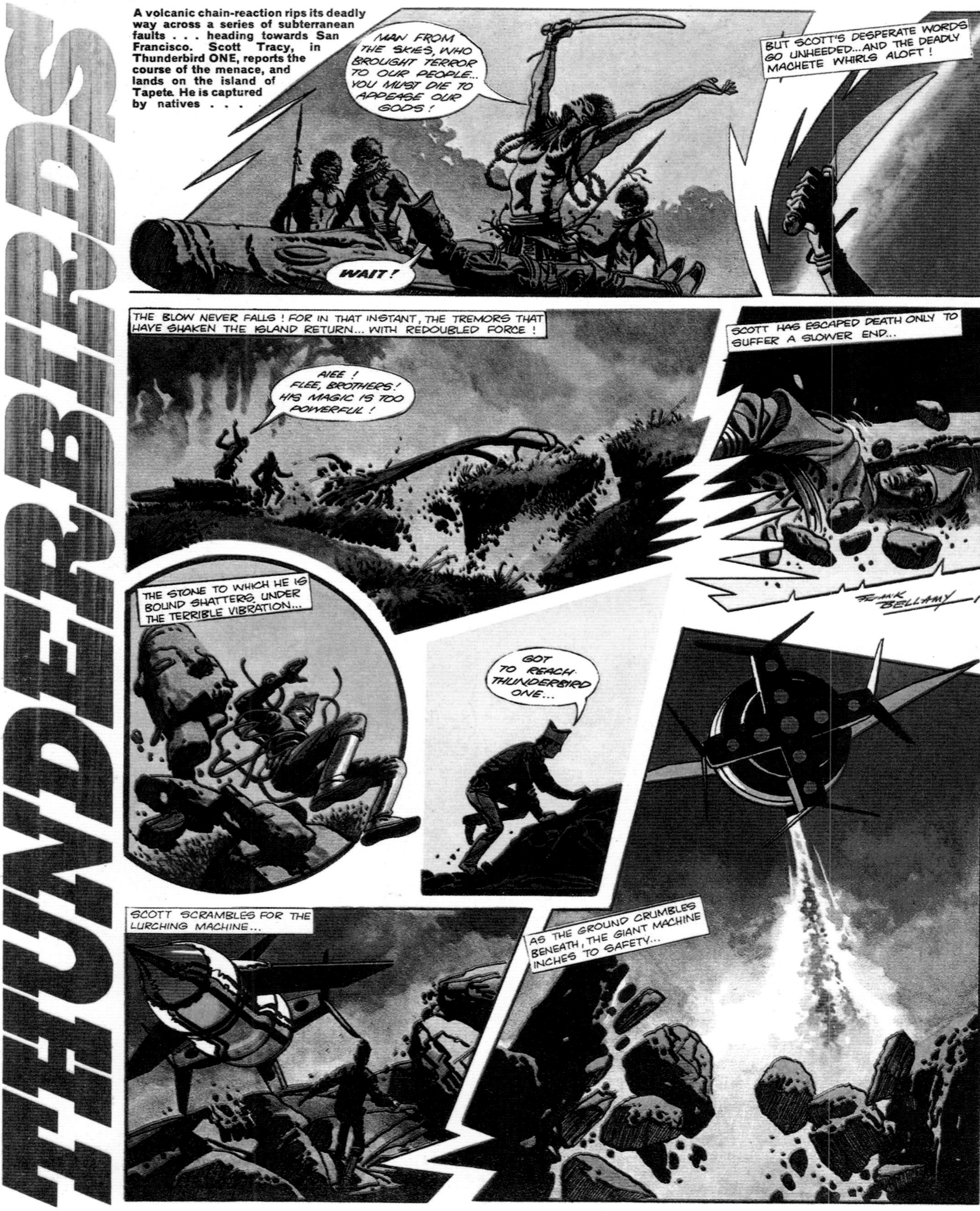
THUNDERBIRDS
A volcanic chain-reaction rips its deadly way across a series of subterranean faults . . . heading towards San Francisco. Scott Tracy, in Thunderbird ONE, reports the course of the menace, and lands on the island of Tapete. He is captured by natives . . .
MAN FROM THE SKIES, WHO BROUGHT TERROR TO OUR PEOPLE... YOU MUST DIE TO APPEASE OUR GODS!
WAIT!
BUT SCOTT'S DESPERATE WORDS GO UNHEEDED...AND THE DEADLY MACHETE WHIRLS ALOFT!
THE BLOW NEVER FALLS! FOR IN THAT INSTANT, THE TREMORS THAT HAVE SHAKEN THE ISLAND RETURN... WITH REDOUBLED FORCE!
AIEE! FLEE, BROTHERS! HIS MAGIC IS TOO POWERFUL!
SCOTT HAS ESCAPED DEATH ONLY TO SUFFER A SLOWER END...
FRANK BELLAMY
THE STONE TO WHICH HE IS BOUND SHATTERS UNDER THE TERRIBLE VIBRATION...
GOT TO REACH THUNDERBIRD ONE...
SCOTT SCRAMBLES FOR THE LURCHING MACHINE...
AS THE GROUND CRUMBLES BENEATH, THE GIANT MACHINE INCHES TO SAFETY...

Artist: Frank Bellamy

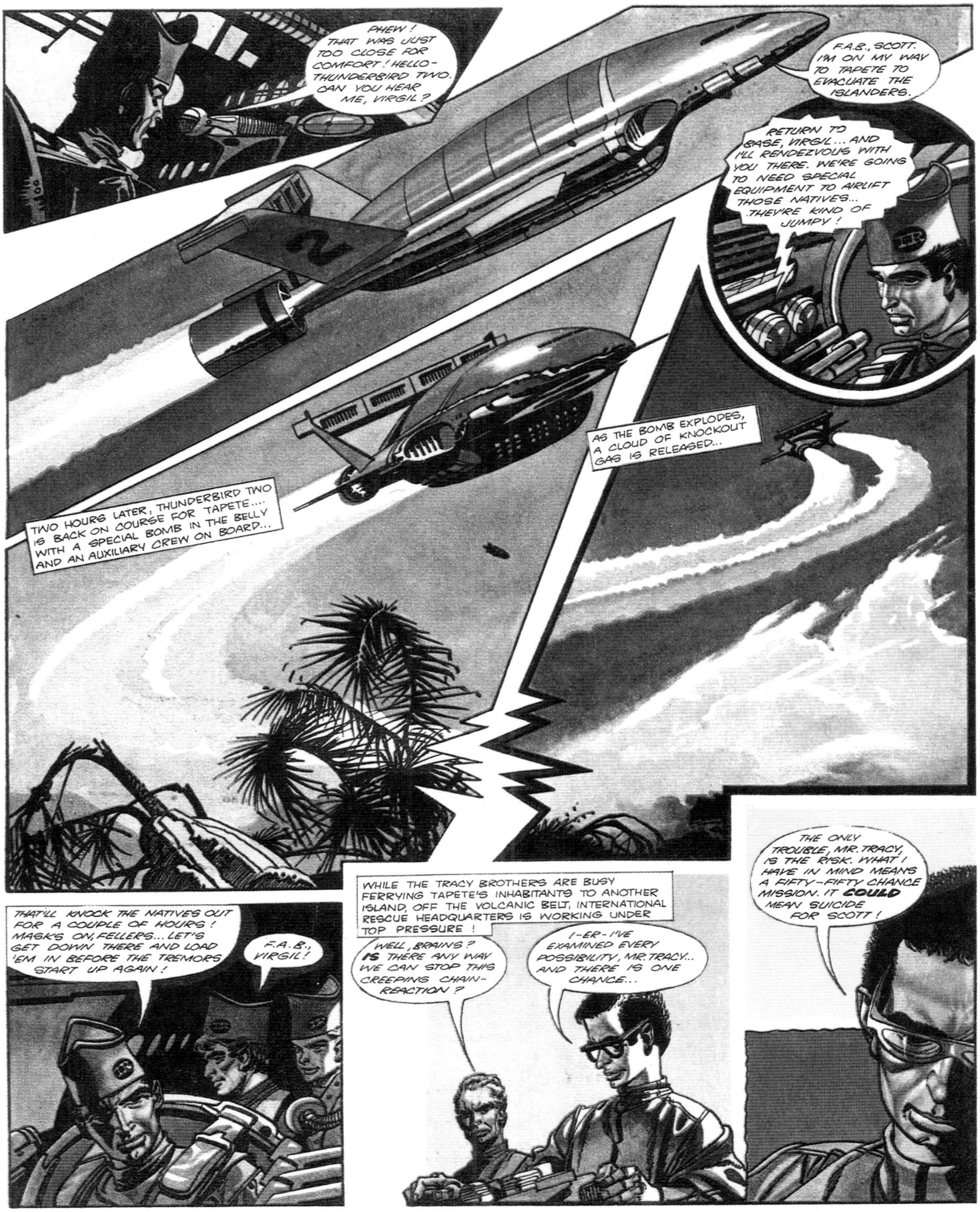
PHEW! THAT WAS JUST TOO CLOSE FOR COMFORT! HELLO-THUNDERBIRD TWO. CAN YOU HEAR ME, VIRGIL?
F.A.B., SCOTT. I'M ON MY WAY TO TAPETE TO EVACUATE THE ISLANDERS.
RETURN TO BASE, VIRGIL... AND I'LL RENDEZVOUS WITH YOU THERE. WE'RE GOING TO NEED SPECIAL EQUIPMENT TO AIRLIFT THOSE NATIVES... THEY'RE KIND OF JUMPY!
TWO HOURS LATER, THUNDERBIRD TWO IS BACK ON COURSE FOR TAPETE.... WITH A SPECIAL BOMB IN THE BELLY AND AN AUXILIARY CREW ON BOARD...
AS THE BOMB EXPLODES, A CLOUD OF KNOCKOUT GAS IS RELEASED...
THAT'LL KNOCK THE NATIVES OUT FOR A COUPLE OF HOURS! MASKS ON, FELLERS... LET'S GET DOWN THERE AND LOAD 'EM IN BEFORE THE TREMORS START UP AGAIN!
F.A.B., VIRGIL!
WHILE THE TRACY BROTHERS ARE BUSY FERRYING TAPETE'S INHABITANTS TO ANOTHER ISLAND, OFF THE VOLCANIC BELT, INTERNATIONAL RESCUE HEADQUARTERS IS WORKING UNDER TOP PRESSURE!
WELL, BRAINS? IS THERE ANY WAY WE CAN STOP THIS CREEPING CHAIN-REACTION?
I-ER-I'VE EXAMINED EVERY POSSIBILITY, MR. TRACY... AND THERE IS ONE CHANCE...
THE ONLY TROUBLE, MR. TRACY, IS THE RISK. WHAT I HAVE IN MIND MEANS A FIFTY-FIFTY CHANCE MISSION. IT COULD MEAN SUICIDE FOR SCOTT!

Part 6 - dateline 28 June 2069

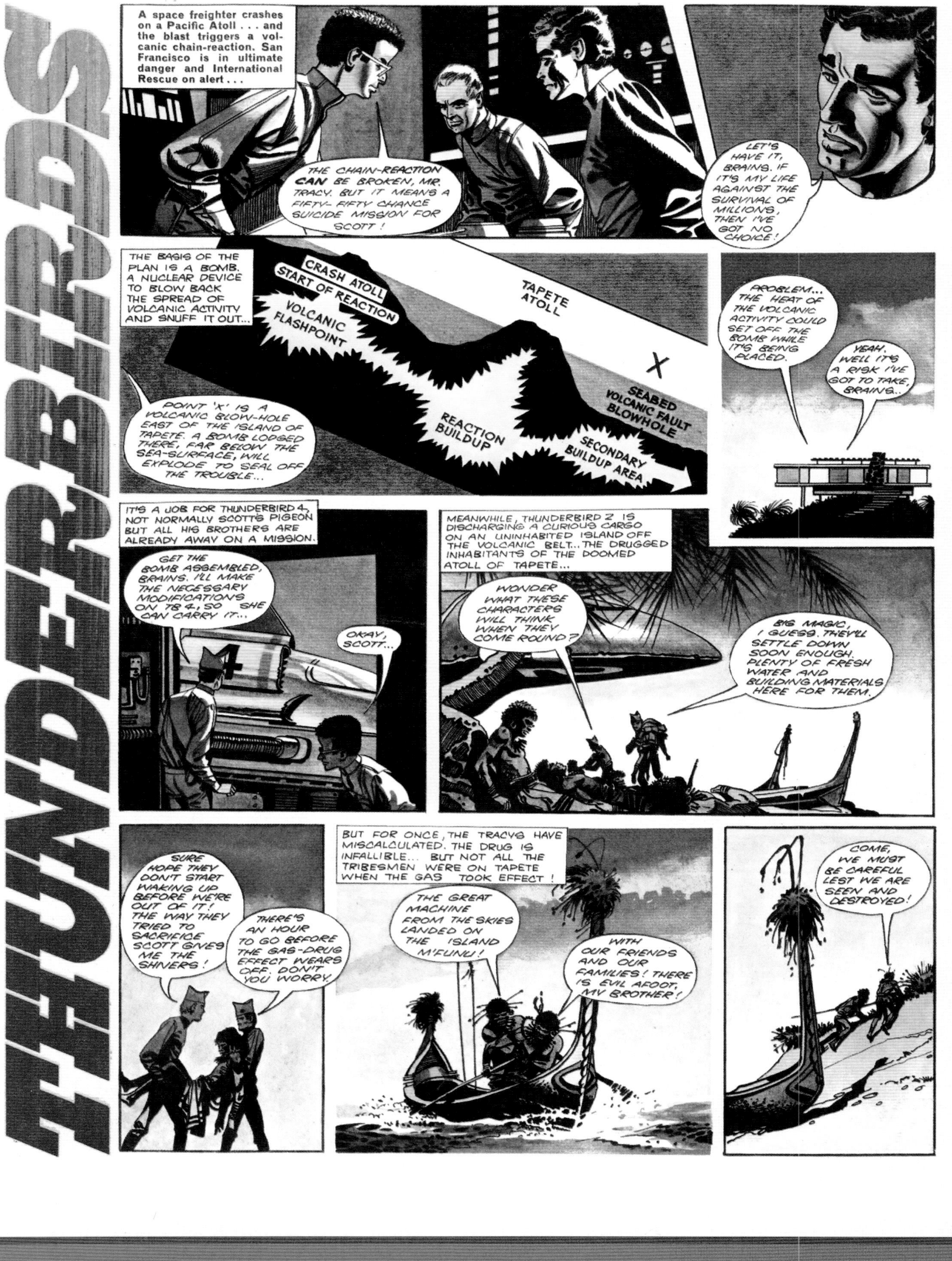
THUNDERBIRDS
A space freighter crashes on a Pacific Atoll . . . and the blast triggers a volcanic chain-reaction. San Francisco is in ultimate danger and International Rescue on alert . . .
THE CHAIN-REACTION CAN BE BROKEN, MR. TRACY. BUT IT MEANS A FIFTY-FIFTY CHANCE SUICIDE MISSION FOR SCOTT!
LET'S HAVE IT, BRAINS. IF IT'S MY LIFE AGAINST THE SURVIVAL OF MILLIONS, THEN I'VE GOT NO CHOICE!
THE BASIS OF THE PLAN IS A BOMB. A NUCLEAR DEVICE TO BLOW BACK THE SPREAD OF VOLCANIC ACTIVITY AND SNUFF IT OUT...
CRASH ATOLL
START OF REACTION
VOLCANIC FLASHPOINT
TAPETE ATOLL
X
SEABED VOLCANIC FAULT BLOWHOLE
REACTION BUILDUP
SECONDARY BUILDUP AREA
POINT 'X' IS A VOLCANIC BLOW-HOLE EAST OF THE ISLAND OF TAPETE. A BOMB LODGED THERE, FAR BELOW THE SEA-SURFACE, WILL EXPLODE TO SEAL OFF THE TROUBLE...
PROBLEM... THE HEAT OF THE VOLCANIC ACTIVITY COULD SET OFF THE BOMB WHILE IT'S BEING PLACED.
YEAH. WELL IT'S A RISK I'VE GOT TO TAKE, BRAINS..
IT'S A JOB FOR THUNDERBIRD 4, NOT NORMALLY SCOTT'S PIGEON BUT ALL HIS BROTHERS ARE ALREADY AWAY ON A MISSION.
GET THE BOMB ASSEMBLED, BRAINS. I'LL MAKE THE NECESSARY MODIFICATIONS ON TB 4, SO SHE CAN CARRY IT...
OKAY, SCOTT...
MEANWHILE, THUNDERBIRD 2 IS DISCHARGING A CURIOUS CARGO ON AN UNINHABITED ISLAND OFF THE VOLCANIC BELT... THE DRUGGED INHABITANTS OF THE DOOMED ATOLL OF TAPETE...
WONDER WHAT THESE CHARACTERS WILL THINK WHEN THEY COME ROUND?
BIG MAGIC, I GUESS. THEY'LL SETTLE DOWN SOON ENOUGH. PLENTY OF FRESH WATER AND BUILDING MATERIALS HERE FOR THEM.
SURE HOPE THEY DON'T START WAKING UP BEFORE WE'RE OUT OF IT! THE WAY THEY TRIED TO SACRIFICE SCOTT GIVES ME THE SHIVERS!
THERE'S AN HOUR TO GO BEFORE THE GAS-DRUG EFFECT WEARS OFF. DON'T YOU WORRY.
BUT FOR ONCE, THE TRACYS HAVE MISCALCULATED. THE DRUG IS INFALLIBLE... BUT NOT ALL THE TRIBESMEN WERE ON TAPETE WHEN THE GAS TOOK EFFECT!
THE GREAT MACHINE FROM THE SKIES LANDED ON THE ISLAND M'FUNU!
WITH OUR FRIENDS AND OUR FAMILIES! THERE IS EVIL AFOOT, MY BROTHER!
COME, WE MUST BE CAREFUL LEST WE ARE SEEN AND DESTROYED!

Artist: Frank Bellamy

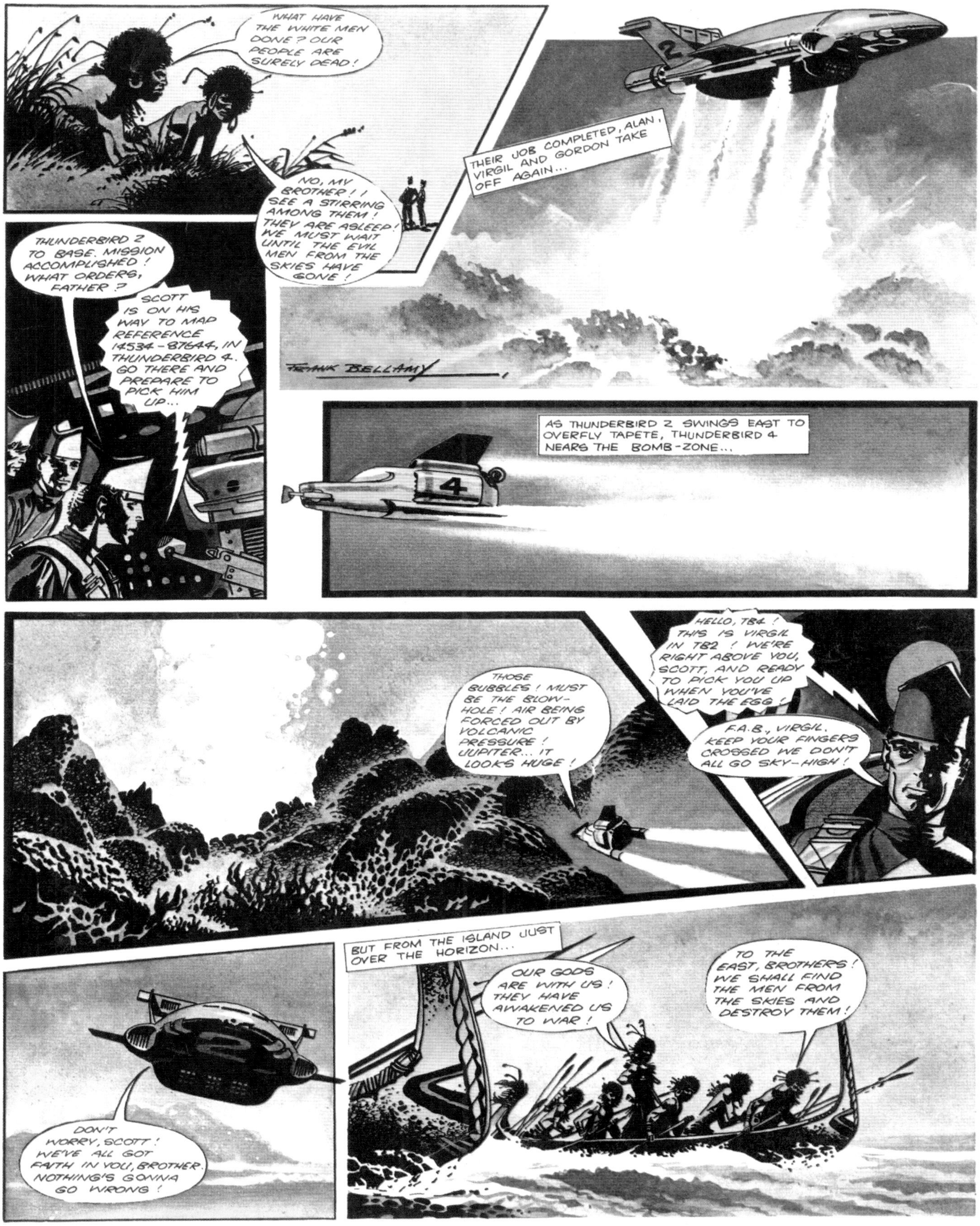
WHAT HAVE THE WHITE MEN DONE? OUR PEOPLE ARE SURELY DEAD!
NO, MY BROTHER! I SEE A STIRRING AMONG THEM! THEY ARE ASLEEP! WE MUST WAIT UNTIL THE EVIL MEN FROM THE SKIES HAVE GONE!
THEIR JOB COMPLETED, ALAN, VIRGIL AND GORDON TAKE OFF AGAIN...
FRANK BELLAMY
THUNDERBIRD 2 TO BASE. MISSION ACCOMPLISHED! WHAT ORDERS, FATHER?
SCOTT IS ON HIS WAY TO MAP REFERENCE 14534-87644, IN THUNDERBIRD 4. GO THERE AND PREPARE TO PICK HIM UP...
AS THUNDERBIRD 2 SWINGS EAST TO OVERFLY TAPETE, THUNDERBIRD 4 NEARS THE BOMB-ZONE...
THOSE BUBBLES! MUST BE THE BLOW-HOLE! AIR BEING FORCED OUT BY VOLCANIC PRESSURE! JUPITER... IT LOOKS HUGE!
HELLO, TB4! THIS IS VIRGIL IN TB2! WE'RE RIGHT ABOVE YOU, SCOTT, AND READY TO PICK YOU UP WHEN YOU'VE LAID THE EGG!
F.A.B., VIRGIL. KEEP YOUR FINGERS CROSSED WE DON'T ALL GO SKY-HIGH!
DON'T WORRY, SCOTT! WE'VE ALL GOT FAITH IN YOU, BROTHER. NOTHING'S GONNA GO WRONG!
BUT FROM THE ISLAND JUST OVER THE HORIZON...
OUR GODS ARE WITH US! THEY HAVE AWAKENED US TO WAR!
TO THE EAST, BROTHERS! WE SHALL FIND THE MEN FROM THE SKIES AND DESTROY THEM!

THUNDERBIRDS

Part 7 - dateline 05 July 2069

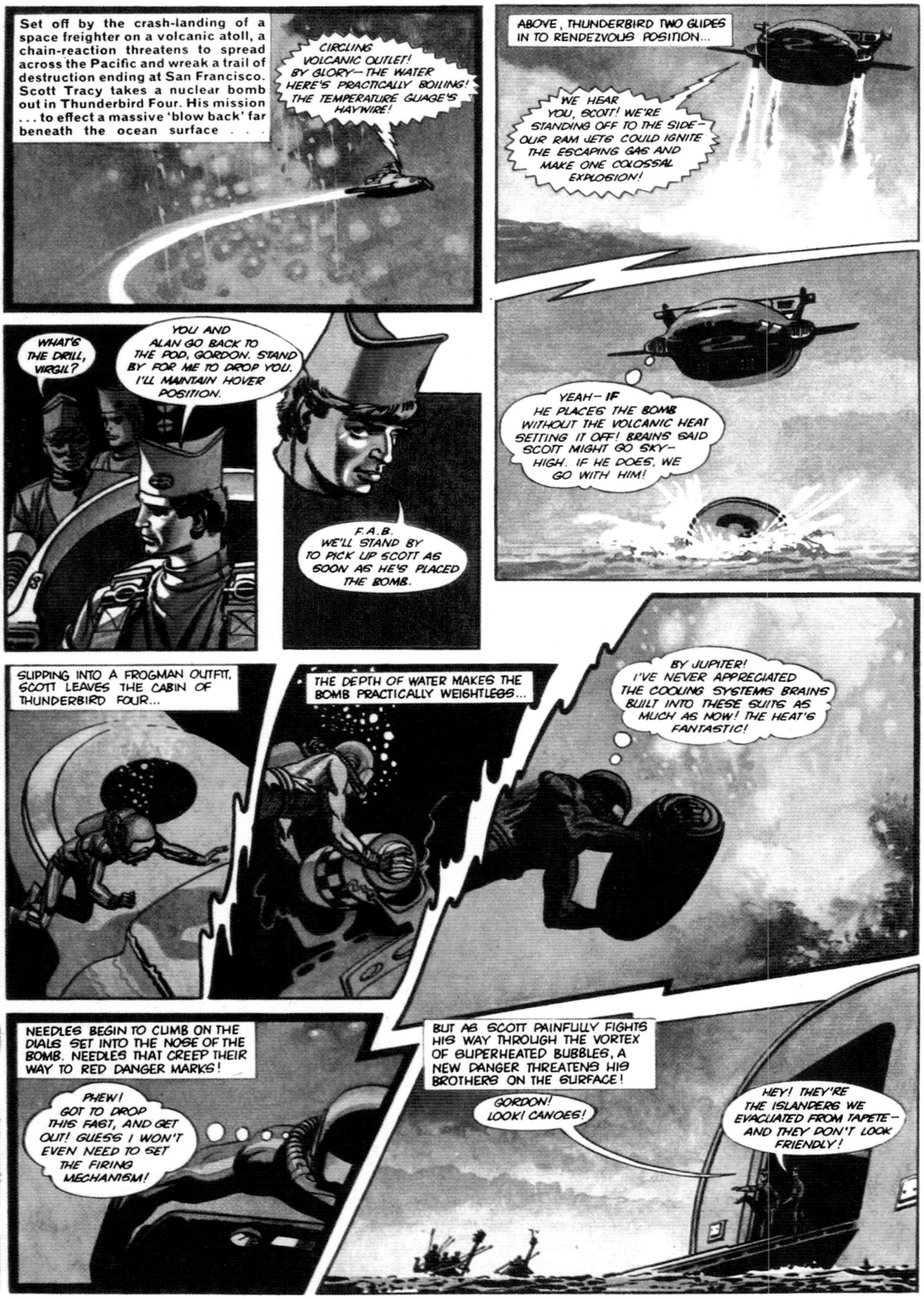
Set off by the crash-landing of a space freighter on a volcanic atoll, a chain-reaction threatens to spread across the Pacific and wreak a trail of destruction ending at San Francisco. Scott Tracy takes a nuclear bomb out in Thunderbird Four. His mission . . . to effect a massive 'blow back' far beneath the ocean surface . . .
CIRCLING VOLCANIC OUTLET! BY GLORY—THE WATER HERE'S PRACTICALLY BOILING! THE TEMPERATURE GUAGE'S HAYWIRE!
ABOVE, THUNDERBIRD TWO GLIDES IN TO RENDEZVOUS POSITION...
WE HEAR YOU, SCOTT! WE'RE STANDING OFF TO THE SIDE—OUR RAM JETS COULD IGNITE THE ESCAPING GAS AND MAKE ONE COLOSSAL EXPLOSION!
WHAT'S THE DRILL, VIRGIL?
YOU AND ALAN GO BACK TO THE POD, GORDON. STAND BY FOR ME TO DROP YOU. I'LL MAINTAIN HOVER POSITION.
F.A.B. WE'LL STAND BY TO PICK UP SCOTT AS SOON AS HE'S PLACED THE BOMB.
YEAH—IF HE PLACES THE BOMB WITHOUT THE VOLCANIC HEAT SETTING IT OFF! BRAINS SAID SCOTT MIGHT GO SKY-HIGH. IF HE DOES, WE GO WITH HIM!
SLIPPING INTO A FROGMAN OUTFIT, SCOTT LEAVES THE CABIN OF THUNDERBIRD FOUR...
THE DEPTH OF WATER MAKES THE BOMB PRACTICALLY WEIGHTLESS...
BY JUPITER! I'VE NEVER APPRECIATED THE COOLING SYSTEMS BRAINS BUILT INTO THESE SUITS AS MUCH AS NOW! THE HEAT'S FANTASTIC!
NEEDLES BEGIN TO CLIMB ON THE DIALS SET INTO THE NOSE OF THE BOMB. NEEDLES THAT CREEP THEIR WAY TO RED DANGER MARKS!
PHEW! GOT TO DROP THIS FAST, AND GET OUT! GUESS I WON'T EVEN NEED TO SET THE FIRING MECHANISM!
BUT AS SCOTT PAINFULLY FIGHTS HIS WAY THROUGH THE VORTEX OF SUPERHEATED BUBBLES, A NEW DANGER THREATENS HIS BROTHERS ON THE SURFACE!
GORDON! LOOK! CANOES!
HEY! THEY'RE THE ISLANDERS WE EVACUATED FROM TAPETE—AND THEY DON'T LOOK FRIENDLY!

Artist: Frank Bellamy

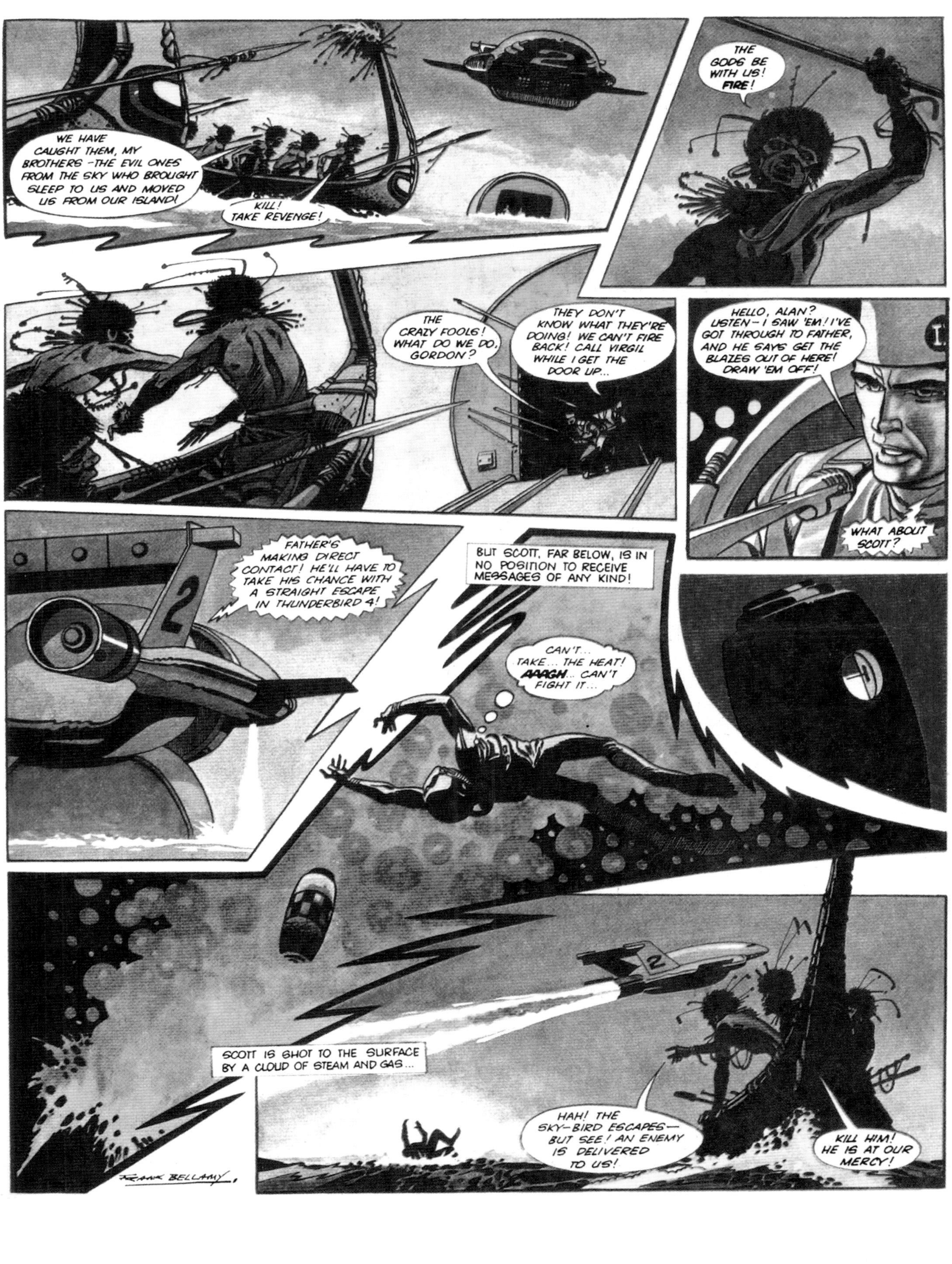
WE HAVE CAUGHT THEM, MY BROTHERS -THE EVIL ONES FROM THE SKY WHO BROUGHT SLEEP TO US AND MOVED US FROM OUR ISLAND!
KILL! TAKE REVENGE!
THE GODS BE WITH US! FIRE!
THE CRAZY FOOLS! WHAT DO WE DO, GORDON?
THEY DON'T KNOW WHAT THEY'RE DOING! WE CAN'T FIRE BACK! CALL VIRGIL WHILE I GET THE DOOR UP...
HELLO, ALAN? LISTEN – I SAW 'EM! I'VE GOT THROUGH TO FATHER, AND HE SAYS GET THE BLAZES OUT OF HERE! DRAW 'EM OFF!
WHAT ABOUT SCOTT?
FATHER'S MAKING DIRECT CONTACT! HE'LL HAVE TO TAKE HIS CHANCE WITH A STRAIGHT ESCAPE IN THUNDERBIRD 4!
BUT SCOTT, FAR BELOW, IS IN NO POSITION TO RECEIVE MESSAGES OF ANY KIND!
CAN'T... TAKE... THE HEAT! AAAGH... CAN'T FIGHT IT...
SCOTT IS SHOT TO THE SURFACE BY A CLOUD OF STEAM AND GAS...
HAH! THE SKY-BIRD ESCAPES– BUT SEE! AN ENEMY IS DELIVERED TO US!
KILL HIM! HE IS AT OUR MERCY!
FRANK BELLAMY

THUNDERBIRDS

Part 8 - dateline 12 July 2069

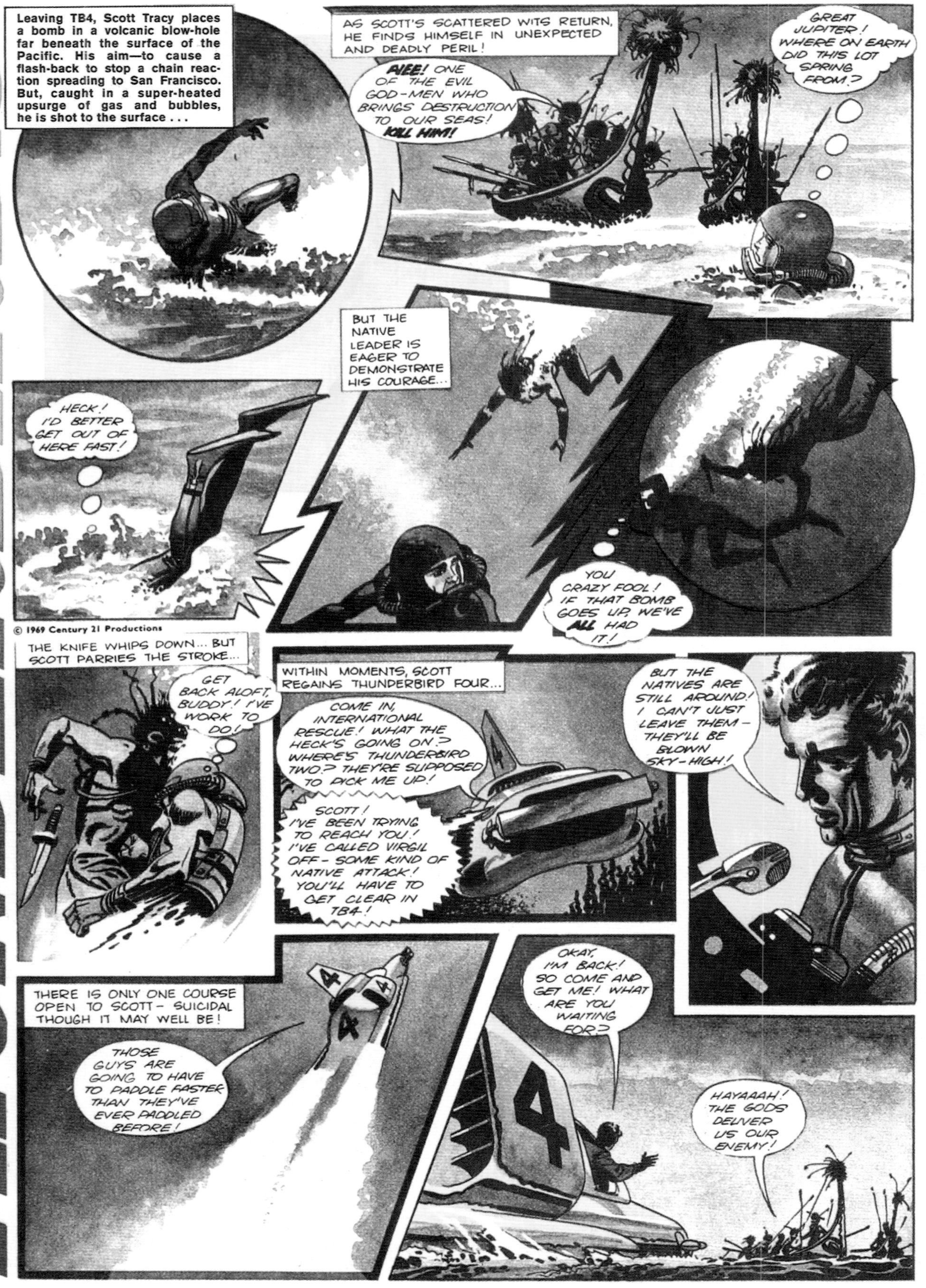
Leaving TB4, Scott Tracy places a bomb in a volcanic blow-hole far beneath the surface of the Pacific. His aim—to cause a flash-back to stop a chain reaction spreading to San Francisco. But, caught in a super-heated upsurge of gas and bubbles, he is shot to the surface . . .
AS SCOTT'S SCATTERED WITS RETURN, HE FINDS HIMSELF IN UNEXPECTED AND DEADLY PERIL!
AIEE! ONE OF THE EVIL GOD-MEN WHO BRINGS DESTRUCTION TO OUR SEAS! KILL HIM!
GREAT JUPITER! WHERE ON EARTH DID THIS LOT SPRING FROM?
HECK! I'D BETTER GET OUT OF HERE FAST!
BUT THE NATIVE LEADER IS EAGER TO DEMONSTRATE HIS COURAGE...
YOU CRAZY FOOL! IF THAT BOMB GOES UP, WE'VE ALL HAD IT!
THE KNIFE WHIPS DOWN... BUT SCOTT PARRIES THE STROKE...
GET BACK ALOFT, BUDDY! I'VE WORK TO DO!
WITHIN MOMENTS, SCOTT REGAINS THUNDERBIRD FOUR...
COME IN, INTERNATIONAL RESCUE! WHAT THE HECK'S GOING ON? WHERE'S THUNDERBIRD TWO? THEY'RE SUPPOSED TO PICK ME UP!
SCOTT! I'VE BEEN TRYING TO REACH YOU! I'VE CALLED VIRGIL OFF - SOME KIND OF NATIVE ATTACK! YOU'LL HAVE TO GET CLEAR IN TB4!
BUT THE NATIVES ARE STILL AROUND! I CAN'T JUST LEAVE THEM - THEY'LL BE BLOWN SKY-HIGH!
THERE IS ONLY ONE COURSE OPEN TO SCOTT - SUICIDAL THOUGH IT MAY WELL BE!
THOSE GUYS ARE GOING TO HAVE TO PADDLE FASTER THAN THEY'VE EVER PADDLED BEFORE!
OKAY, I'M BACK! SO COME AND GET ME! WHAT ARE YOU WAITING FOR?
HAYAAAH! THE GODS DELIVER US OUR ENEMY!

Artist: Frank Bellamy

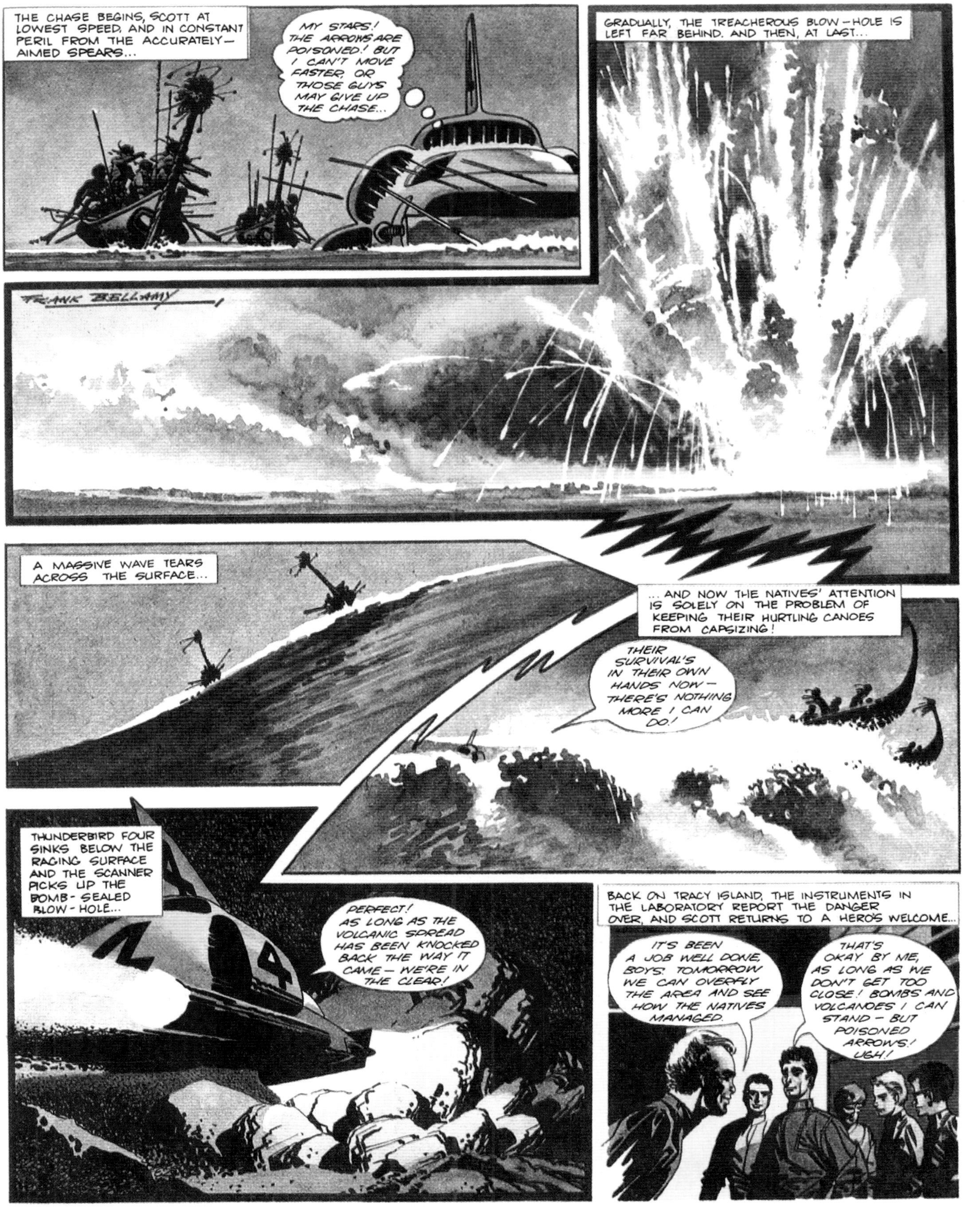
THE CHASE BEGINS, SCOTT AT LOWEST SPEED, AND IN CONSTANT PERIL FROM THE ACCURATELY-AIMED SPEARS...
MY STARS! THE ARROWS ARE POISONED! BUT I CAN'T MOVE FASTER, OR THOSE GUYS MAY GIVE UP THE CHASE...
GRADUALLY, THE TREACHEROUS BLOW-HOLE IS LEFT FAR BEHIND. AND THEN, AT LAST...
FRANK BELLAMY
A MASSIVE WAVE TEARS ACROSS THE SURFACE...
...AND NOW THE NATIVES' ATTENTION IS SOLELY ON THE PROBLEM OF KEEPING THEIR HURTLING CANOES FROM CAPSIZING!
THEIR SURVIVAL'S IN THEIR OWN HANDS NOW— THERE'S NOTHING MORE I CAN DO!
THUNDERBIRD FOUR SINKS BELOW THE RAGING SURFACE AND THE SCANNER PICKS UP THE BOMB-SEALED BLOW-HOLE...
PERFECT! AS LONG AS THE VOLCANIC SPREAD HAS BEEN KNOCKED BACK THE WAY IT CAME— WE'RE IN THE CLEAR!
BACK ON TRACY ISLAND, THE INSTRUMENTS IN THE LABORATORY REPORT THE DANGER OVER, AND SCOTT RETURNS TO A HERO'S WELCOME...
IT'S BEEN A JOB WELL DONE, BOYS: TOMORROW WE CAN OVERFLY THE AREA AND SEE HOW THE NATIVES MANAGED.
THAT'S OKAY BY ME, AS LONG AS WE DON'T GET TOO CLOSE! BOMBS AND VOLCANOES I CAN STAND – BUT POISONED ARROWS! UGH!

THUNDERBIRDS

Part 1 - dateline 19 July 2069

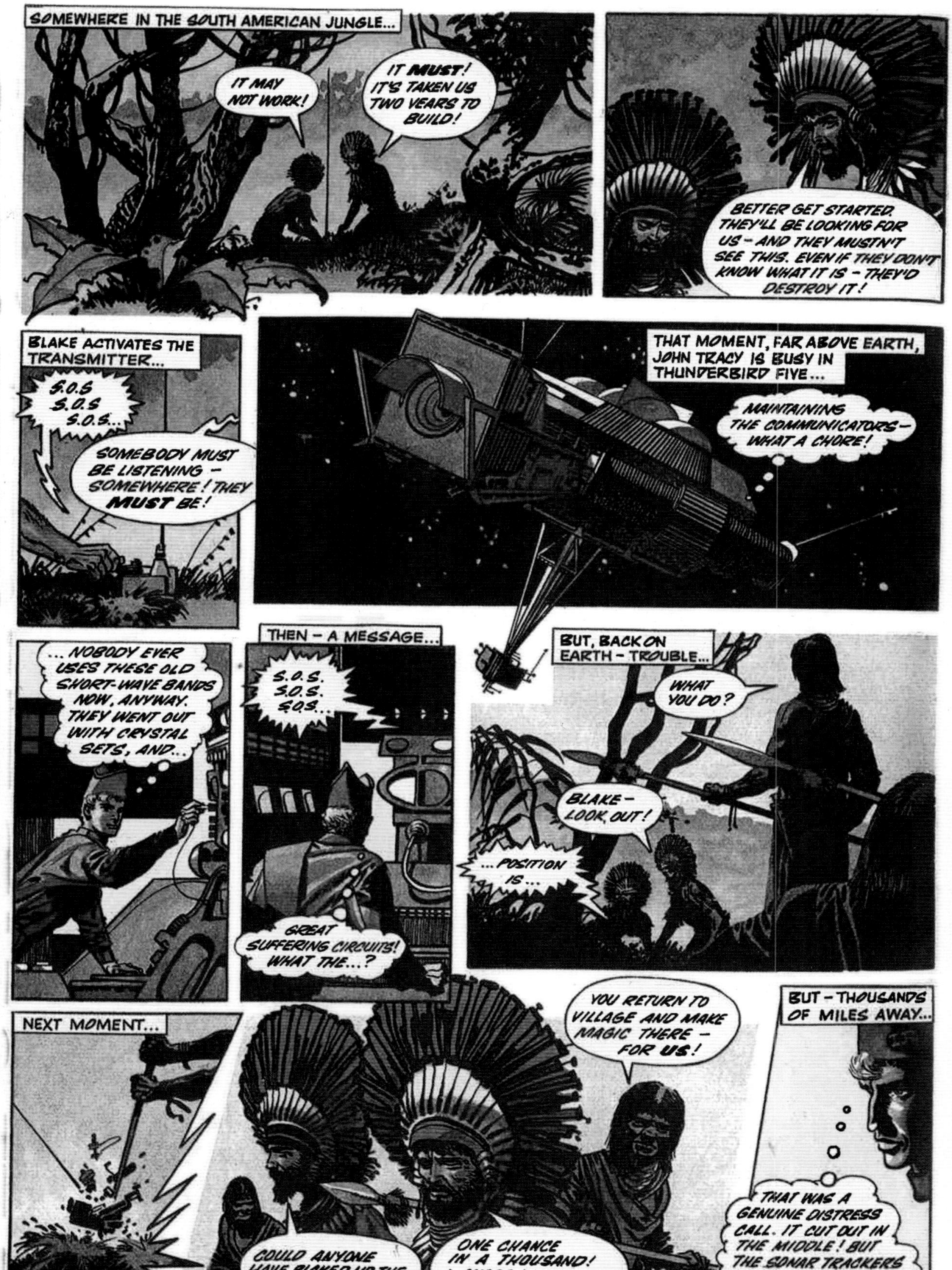
SOMEWHERE IN THE SOUTH AMERICAN JUNGLE...
IT MAY NOT WORK!
IT MUST! IT'S TAKEN US TWO YEARS TO BUILD!
BETTER GET STARTED. THEY'LL BE LOOKING FOR US - AND THEY MUSTN'T SEE THIS. EVEN IF THEY DON'T KNOW WHAT IT IS - THEY'D DESTROY IT!
BLAKE ACTIVATES THE TRANSMITTER...
S.O.S S.O.S S.O.S...
SOMEBODY MUST BE LISTENING - SOMEWHERE! THEY MUST BE!
THAT MOMENT, FAR ABOVE EARTH, JOHN TRACY IS BUSY IN THUNDERBIRD FIVE...
MAINTAINING THE COMMUNICATORS - WHAT A CHORE!
... NOBODY EVER USES THESE OLD SHORT-WAVE BANDS NOW, ANYWAY. THEY WENT OUT WITH CRYSTAL SETS, AND...
THEN - A MESSAGE...
S.O.S. S.O.S. S.O.S...
GREAT SUFFERING CIRCUITS! WHAT THE...?
BUT, BACK ON EARTH - TROUBLE...
WHAT YOU DO?
BLAKE - LOOK OUT!
...POSITION IS...
NEXT MOMENT...
YOU RETURN TO VILLAGE AND MAKE MAGIC THERE - FOR US!
COULD ANYONE HAVE PICKED UP THE SIGNAL YET?
ONE CHANCE IN A THOUSAND! I GUESS WE'RE STUCK HERE FOR LIFE!
BUT - THOUSANDS OF MILES AWAY...
THAT WAS A GENUINE DISTRESS CALL. IT CUT OUT IN THE MIDDLE! BUT THE SONAR TRACKERS WILL HAVE REGISTERED IT...

Artist: Frank Bellamy

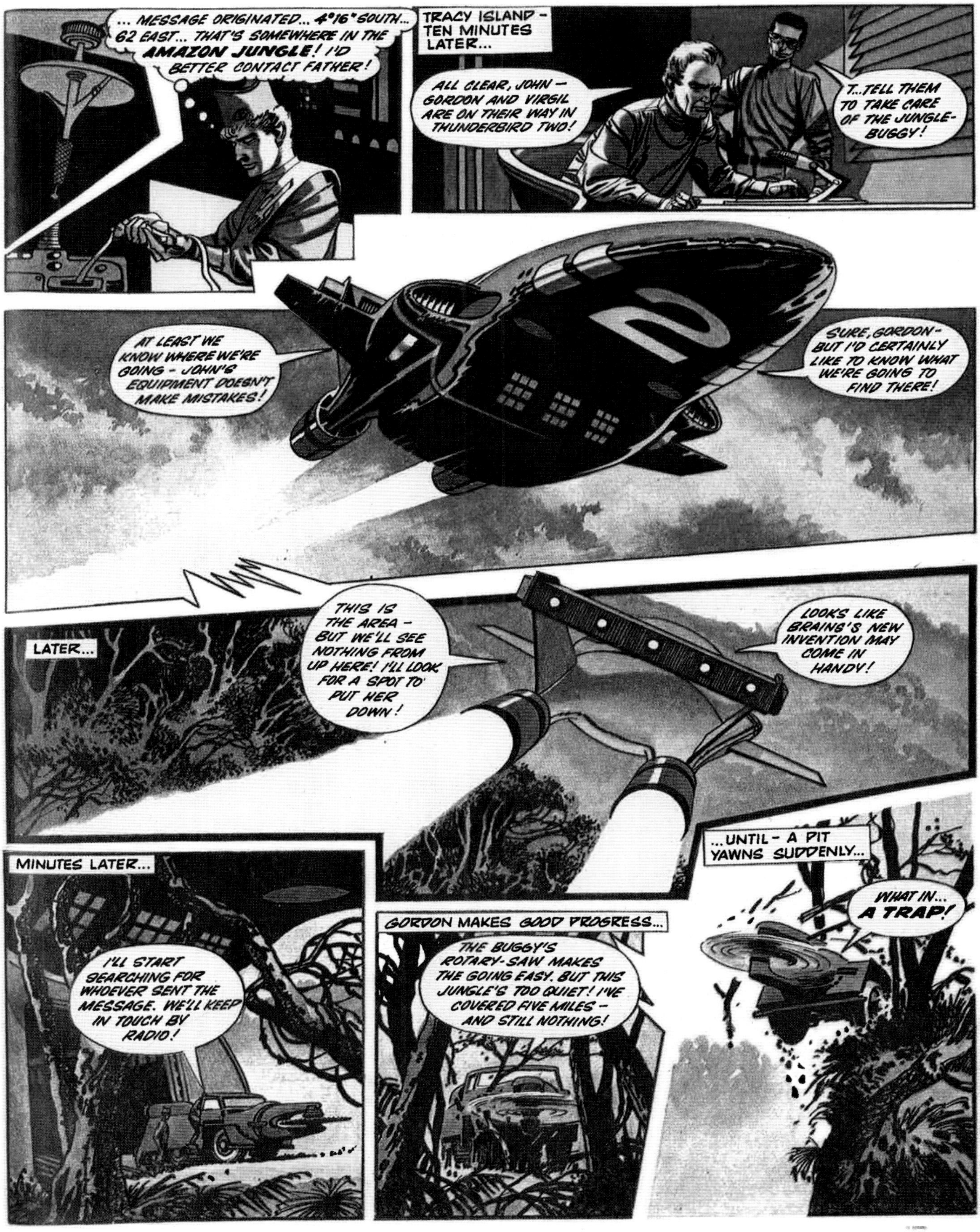
... MESSAGE ORIGINATED... 4°16" SOUTH... 62 EAST... THAT'S SOMEWHERE IN THE AMAZON JUNGLE! I'D BETTER CONTACT FATHER!
TRACY ISLAND - TEN MINUTES LATER...
ALL CLEAR, JOHN - GORDON AND VIRGIL ARE ON THEIR WAY IN THUNDERBIRD TWO!
T...TELL THEM TO TAKE CARE OF THE JUNGLE-BUGGY!
AT LEAST WE KNOW WHERE WE'RE GOING - JOHN'S EQUIPMENT DOESN'T MAKE MISTAKES!
SURE, GORDON - BUT I'D CERTAINLY LIKE TO KNOW WHAT WE'RE GOING TO FIND THERE!
LATER...
THIS IS THE AREA - BUT WE'LL SEE NOTHING FROM UP HERE! I'LL LOOK FOR A SPOT TO PUT HER DOWN!
LOOKS LIKE BRAINS'S NEW INVENTION MAY COME IN HANDY!
MINUTES LATER...
I'LL START SEARCHING FOR WHOEVER SENT THE MESSAGE. WE'LL KEEP IN TOUCH BY RADIO!
GORDON MAKES GOOD PROGRESS...
THE BUGGY'S ROTARY-SAW MAKES THE GOING EASY. BUT THIS JUNGLE'S TOO QUIET! I'VE COVERED FIVE MILES - AND STILL NOTHING!
...UNTIL - A PIT YAWNS SUDDENLY...
WHAT IN... A TRAP!

THUNDERBIRDS

Part 2 - dateline 26 July 2069

Artist: Frank Bellamy

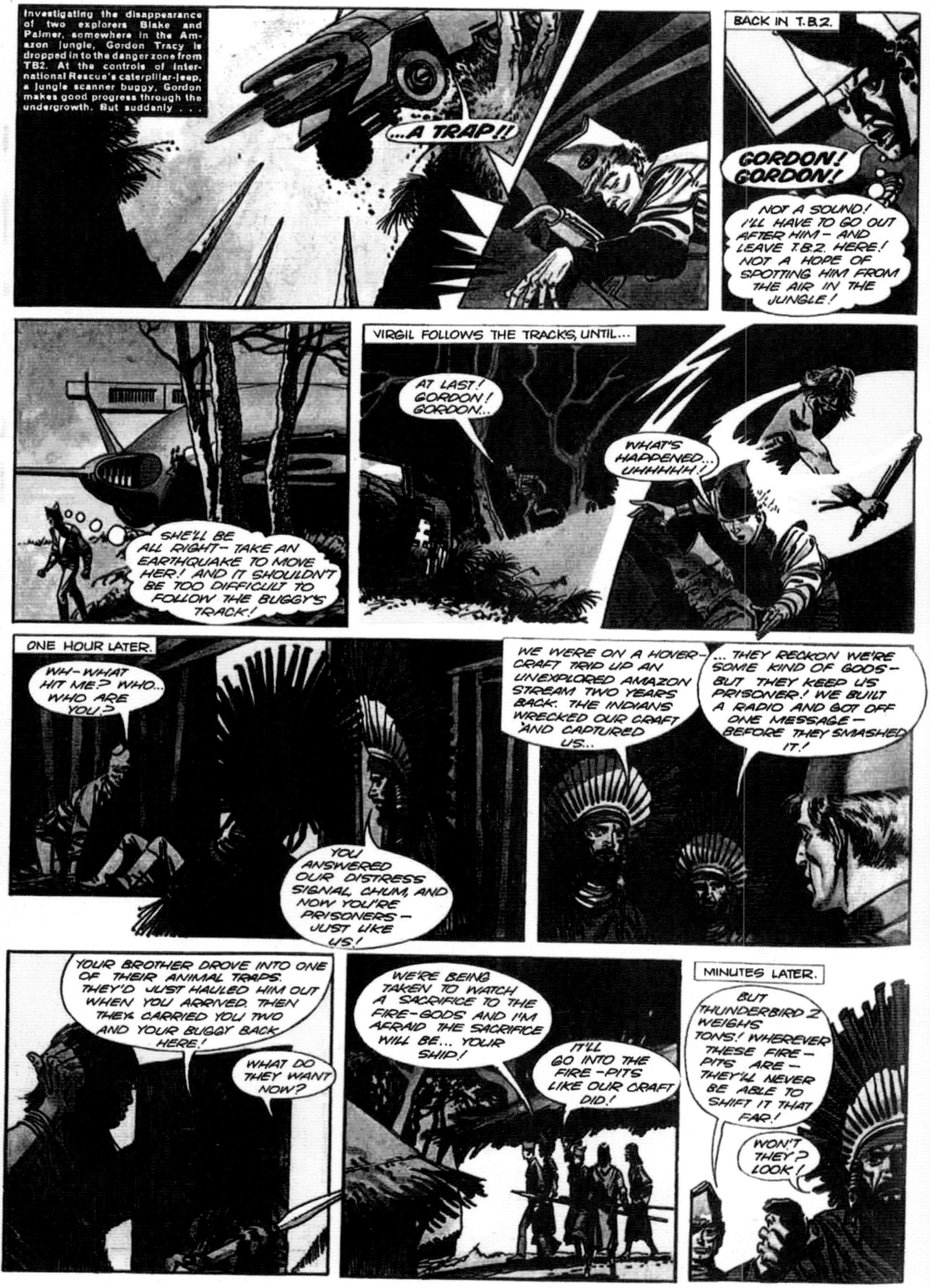
Investigating the disappearance of two explorers Blake and Palmer, somewhere in the Amazon jungle, Gordon Tracy is dropped in to the danger zone from TB2. At the controls of International Rescue's caterpillar-jeep, a jungle scanner buggy, Gordon makes good progress through the undergrowth. But suddenly . . .
...A TRAP!!
BACK IN T.B.2.
GORDON! GORDON!
NOT A SOUND! I'LL HAVE TO GO OUT AFTER HIM – AND LEAVE T.B.2. HERE! NOT A HOPE OF SPOTTING HIM FROM THE AIR IN THE JUNGLE!
SHE'LL BE ALL RIGHT– TAKE AN EARTHQUAKE TO MOVE HER! AND IT SHOULDN'T BE TOO DIFFICULT TO FOLLOW THE BUGGY'S TRACK!
VIRGIL FOLLOWS THE TRACKS, UNTIL...
AT LAST! GORDON! GORDON...
WHAT'S HAPPENED... UHHHHH!
ONE HOUR LATER.
WH-WHAT HIT ME? WHO... WHO ARE YOU?
YOU ANSWERED OUR DISTRESS SIGNAL, CHUM, AND NOW YOU'RE PRISONERS – JUST LIKE US!
WE WERE ON A HOVER-CRAFT TRIP UP AN UNEXPLORED AMAZON STREAM TWO YEARS BACK. THE INDIANS WRECKED OUR CRAFT AND CAPTURED US...
... THEY RECKON WE'RE SOME KIND OF GODS – BUT THEY KEEP US PRISONER! WE BUILT A RADIO AND GOT OFF ONE MESSAGE – BEFORE THEY SMASHED IT!
YOUR BROTHER DROVE INTO ONE OF THEIR ANIMAL TRAPS. THEY'D JUST HAULED HIM OUT WHEN YOU ARRIVED. THEN THEY CARRIED YOU TWO AND YOUR BUGGY BACK HERE!
WHAT DO THEY WANT NOW?
WE'RE BEING TAKEN TO WATCH A SACRIFICE TO THE FIRE-GODS AND I'M AFRAID THE SACRIFICE WILL BE... YOUR SHIP!
IT'LL GO INTO THE FIRE-PITS LIKE OUR CRAFT DID!
MINUTES LATER.
BUT THUNDERBIRD 2 WEIGHS TONS! WHEREVER THESE FIRE-PITS ARE – THEY'LL NEVER BE ABLE TO SHIFT IT THAT FAR!
WON'T THEY? LOOK!

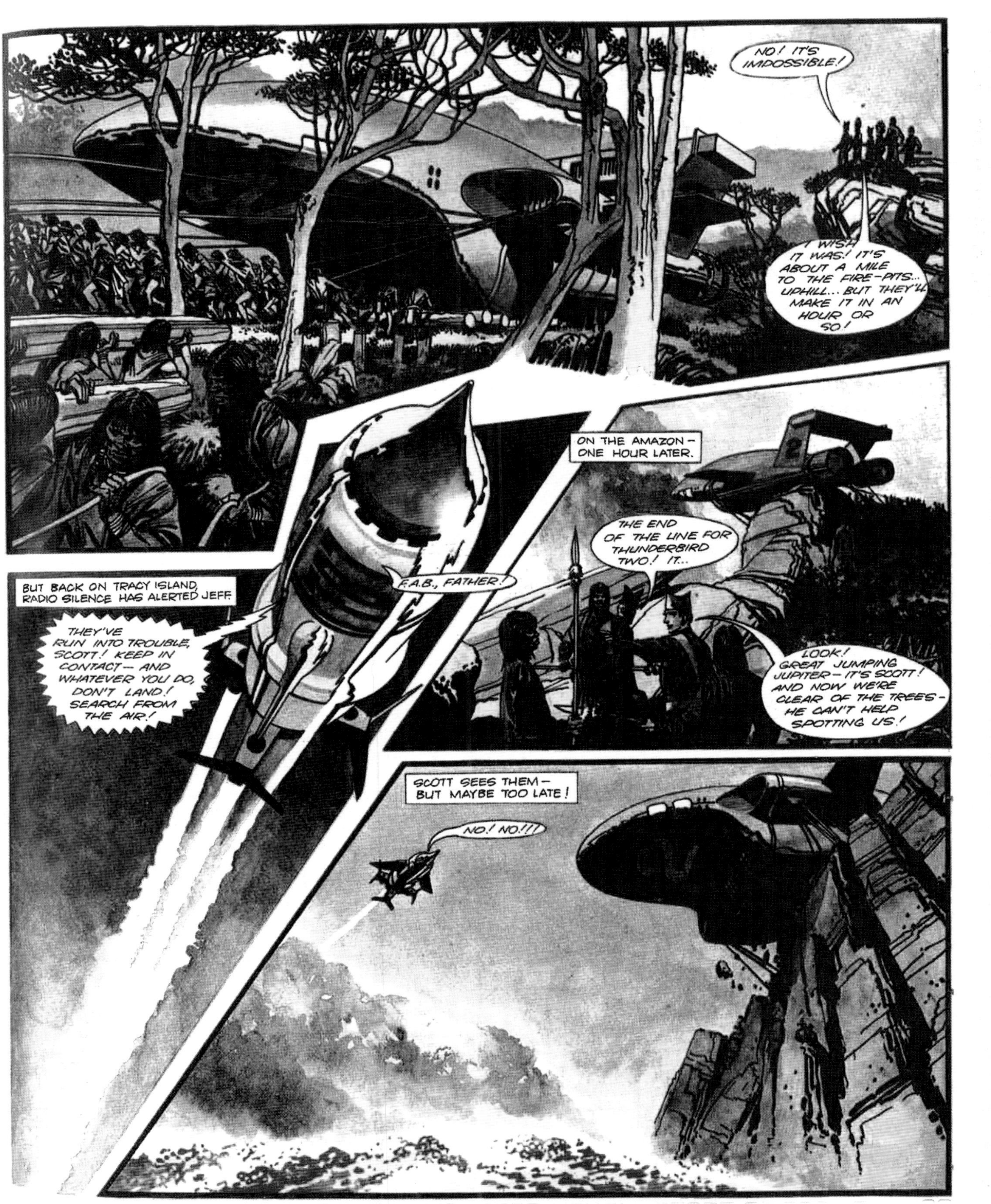
NO! IT'S IMPOSSIBLE!
I WISH IT WAS! IT'S ABOUT A MILE TO THE FIRE-PITS... UPHILL... BUT THEY'LL MAKE IT IN AN HOUR OR SO!
ON THE AMAZON - ONE HOUR LATER.
THE END OF THE LINE FOR THUNDERBIRD TWO! IT...
BUT BACK ON TRACY ISLAND, RADIO SILENCE HAS ALERTED JEFF.
THEY'VE RUN INTO TROUBLE, SCOTT! KEEP IN CONTACT -- AND WHATEVER YOU DO, DON'T LAND! SEARCH FROM THE AIR!
F.A.B., FATHER!
LOOK! GREAT JUMPING JUPITER - IT'S SCOTT! AND NOW WE'RE CLEAR OF THE TREES - HE CAN'T HELP SPOTTING US!
SCOTT SEES THEM - BUT MAYBE TOO LATE!
NO! NO!!!

THUNDERBIRDS

Part 3 - dateline 02 August 2069

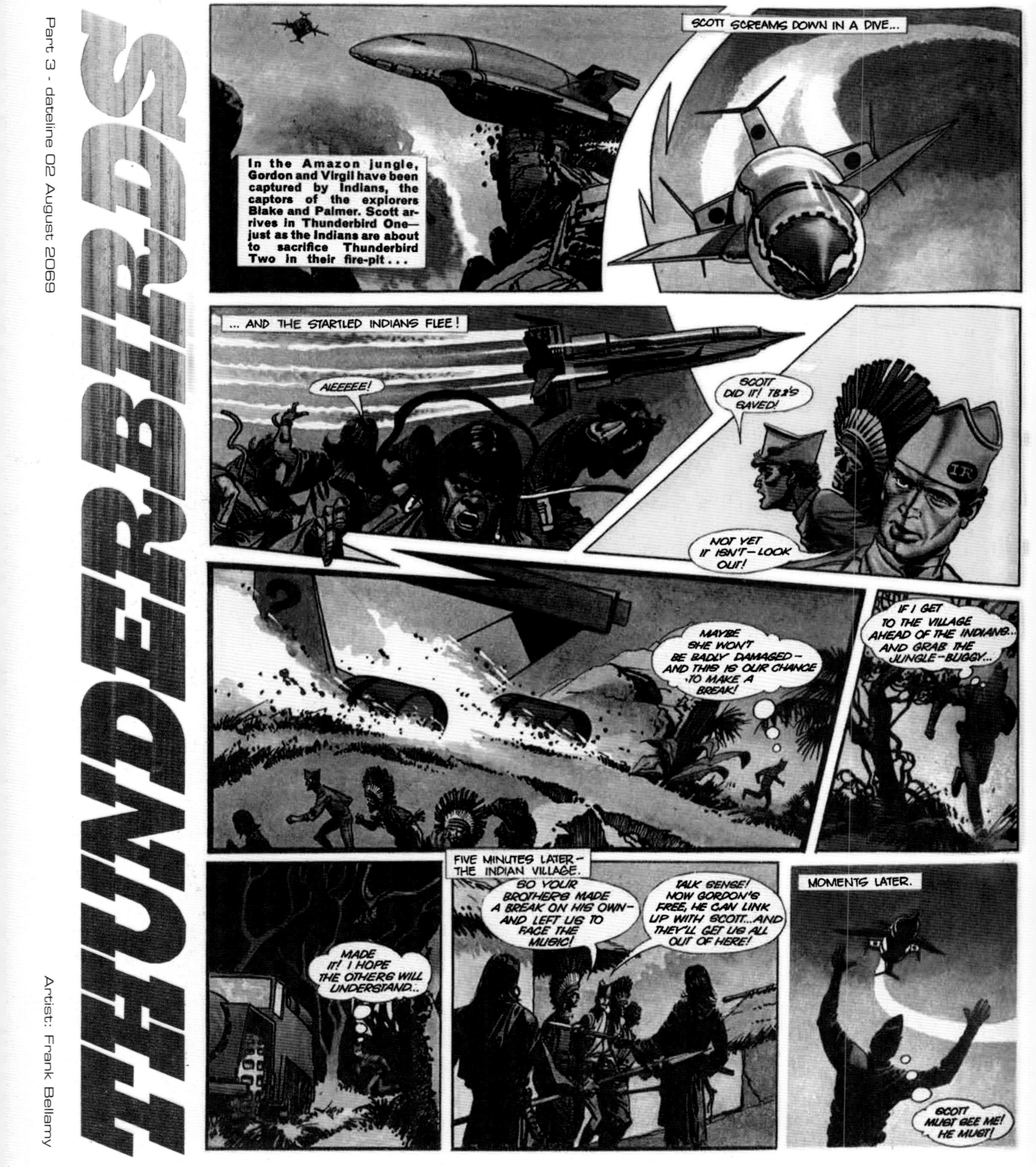
In the Amazon jungle, Gordon and Virgil have been captured by Indians, the captors of the explorers Blake and Palmer. Scott arrives in Thunderbird One—just as the Indians are about to sacrifice Thunderbird Two in their fire-pit . . .
SCOTT SCREAMS DOWN IN A DIVE...
... AND THE STARTLED INDIANS FLEE!
AIEEEEE!
SCOTT DID IT! TB2'S SAVED!
NOT YET IT ISN'T—LOOK OUT!
MAYBE SHE WON'T BE BADLY DAMAGED—AND THIS IS OUR CHANCE TO MAKE A BREAK!
IF I GET TO THE VILLAGE AHEAD OF THE INDIANS... AND GRAB THE JUNGLE-BUGGY...
MADE IT! I HOPE THE OTHERS WILL UNDERSTAND...
FIVE MINUTES LATER—THE INDIAN VILLAGE.
SO YOUR BROTHER'S MADE A BREAK ON HIS OWN—AND LEFT US TO FACE THE MUSIC!
TALK SENSE! NOW GORDON'S FREE, HE CAN LINK UP WITH SCOTT...AND THEY'LL GET US ALL OUT OF HERE!
MOMENTS LATER.
SCOTT MUST SEE ME! HE MUST!

Artist: Frank Bellamy

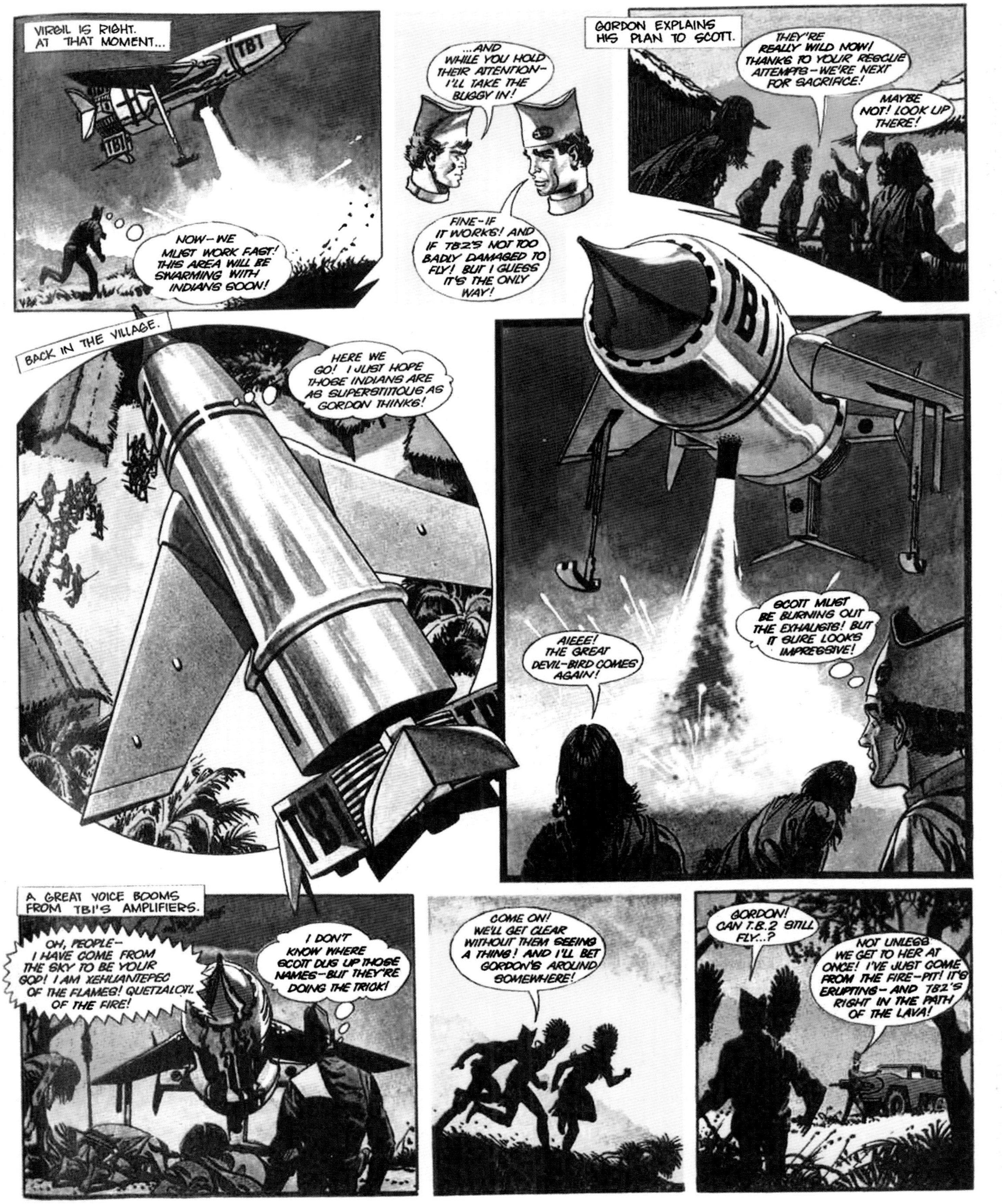
VIRGIL IS RIGHT. AT THAT MOMENT...
NOW—WE MUST WORK FAST! THIS AREA WILL BE SWARMING WITH INDIANS SOON!
...AND WHILE YOU HOLD THEIR ATTENTION—I'LL TAKE THE BUGGY IN!
FINE—IF IT WORKS! AND IF TB2'S NOT TOO BADLY DAMAGED TO FLY! BUT I GUESS IT'S THE ONLY WAY!
GORDON EXPLAINS HIS PLAN TO SCOTT.
THEY'RE REALLY WILD NOW! THANKS TO YOUR RESCUE ATTEMPTS—WE'RE NEXT FOR SACRIFICE!
MAYBE NOT! LOOK UP THERE!
BACK IN THE VILLAGE.
HERE WE GO! I JUST HOPE THOSE INDIANS ARE AS SUPERSTITIOUS AS GORDON THINKS!
AIEEE! THE GREAT DEVIL-BIRD COMES AGAIN!
SCOTT MUST BE BURNING OUT THE EXHAUSTS! BUT IT SURE LOOKS IMPRESSIVE!
A GREAT VOICE BOOMS FROM TB1'S AMPLIFIERS.
OH, PEOPLE—I HAVE COME FROM THE SKY TO BE YOUR GOD! I AM XEHUANTEPEC OF THE FLAMES! QUETZALOTL OF THE FIRE!
I DON'T KNOW WHERE SCOTT DUG UP THOSE NAMES—BUT THEY'RE DOING THE TRICK!
COME ON! WE'LL GET CLEAR WITHOUT THEM SEEING A THING! AND I'LL BET GORDON'S AROUND SOMEWHERE!
GORDON! CAN T.B.2 STILL FLY...?
NOT UNLESS WE GET TO HER AT ONCE! I'VE JUST COME FROM THE FIRE-PIT! IT'S ERUPTING—AND TB2'S RIGHT IN THE PATH OF THE LAVA!

THUNDERBIRDS

Part 4 - dateline 09 August 2069

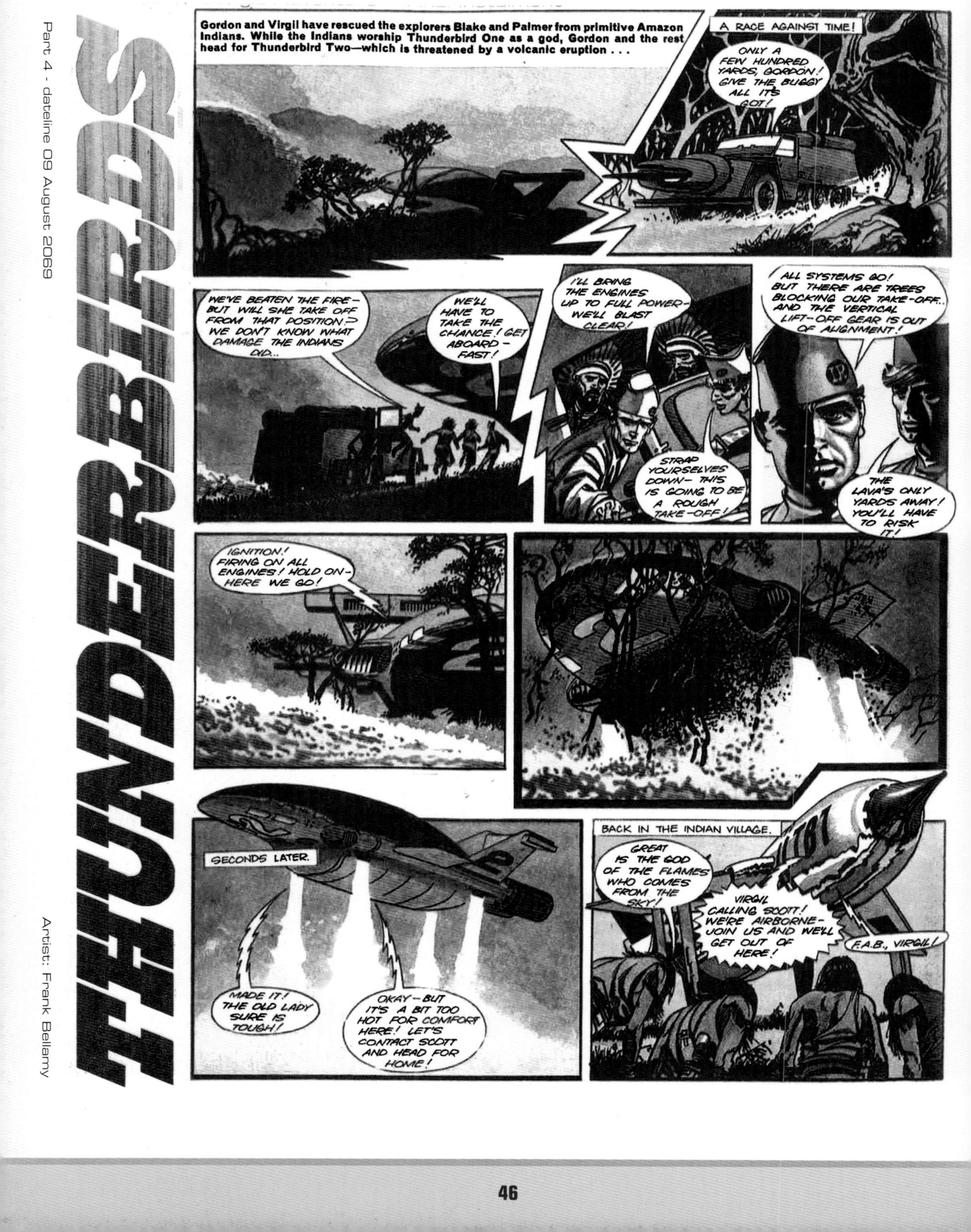
Gordon and Virgil have rescued the explorers Blake and Palmer from primitive Amazon Indians. While the Indians worship Thunderbird One as a god, Gordon and the rest head for Thunderbird Two—which is threatened by a volcanic eruption . . .
A RACE AGAINST TIME!
ONLY A FEW HUNDRED YARDS, GORDON! GIVE THE BUGGY ALL IT'S GOT!
WE'VE BEATEN THE FIRE- BUT WILL SHE TAKE OFF FROM THAT POSITION? WE DON'T KNOW WHAT DAMAGE THE INDIANS DID..
WE'LL HAVE TO TAKE THE CHANCE! GET ABOARD - FAST!
I'LL BRING THE ENGINES UP TO FULL POWER- WE'LL BLAST CLEAR!
STRAP YOURSELVES DOWN- THIS IS GOING TO BE A ROUGH TAKE-OFF!
ALL SYSTEMS GO! BUT THERE ARE TREES BLOCKING OUR TAKE-OFF.. AND THE VERTICAL LIFT-OFF GEAR IS OUT OF ALIGNMENT!
THE LAVA'S ONLY YARDS AWAY! YOU'LL HAVE TO RISK IT!
IGNITION! FIRING ON ALL ENGINES! HOLD ON- HERE WE GO!
SECONDS LATER.
MADE IT! THE OLD LADY SURE IS TOUGH!
OKAY-BUT IT'S A BIT TOO HOT FOR COMFORT HERE! LET'S CONTACT SCOTT AND HEAD FOR HOME!
BACK IN THE INDIAN VILLAGE.
GREAT IS THE GOD OF THE FLAMES WHO COMES FROM THE SKY!
VIRGIL CALLING SCOTT! WE'RE AIRBORNE- JOIN US AND WE'LL GET OUT OF HERE!
F.A.B., VIRGIL!

Artist: Frank Bellamy

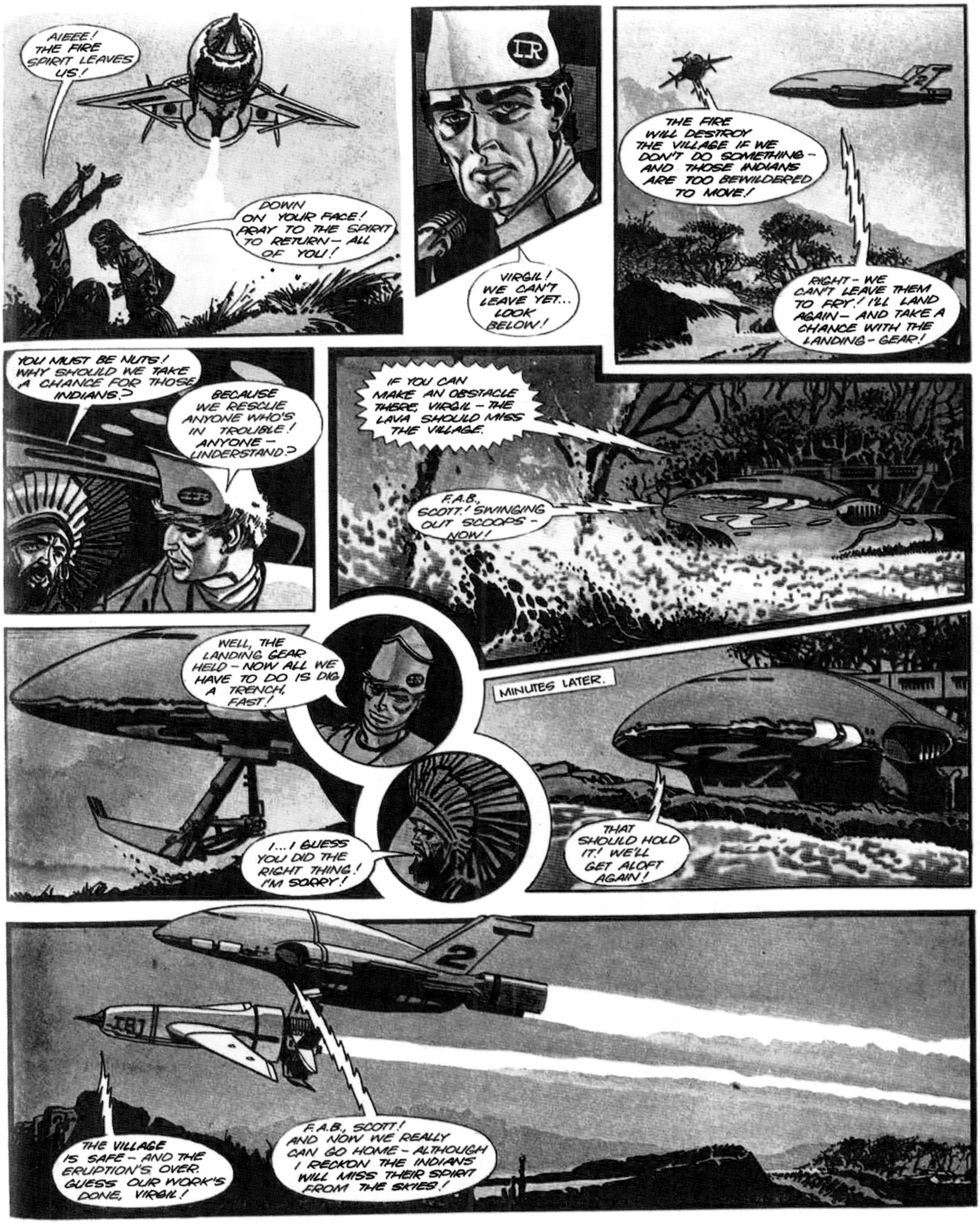
AIEEE! THE FIRE SPIRIT LEAVES US!
DOWN ON YOUR FACE! PRAY TO THE SPIRIT TO RETURN – ALL OF YOU!
VIRGIL! WE CAN'T LEAVE YET... LOOK BELOW!
THE FIRE WILL DESTROY THE VILLAGE IF WE DON'T DO SOMETHING – AND THOSE INDIANS ARE TOO BEWILDERED TO MOVE!
RIGHT – WE CAN'T LEAVE THEM TO FRY! I'LL LAND AGAIN – AND TAKE A CHANCE WITH THE LANDING-GEAR!
YOU MUST BE NUTS! WHY SHOULD WE TAKE A CHANCE FOR THOSE INDIANS?
BECAUSE WE RESCUE ANYONE WHO'S IN TROUBLE! ANYONE – UNDERSTAND?
IF YOU CAN MAKE AN OBSTACLE THERE, VIRGIL – THE LAVA SHOULD MISS THE VILLAGE.
F.A.B., SCOTT! SWINGING OUT SCOOPS – NOW!
WELL, THE LANDING GEAR HELD – NOW ALL WE HAVE TO DO IS DIG A TRENCH, FAST!
I... I GUESS YOU DID THE RIGHT THING! I'M SORRY!
MINUTES LATER.
THAT SHOULD HOLD IT! WE'LL GET ALOFT AGAIN!
THE VILLAGE IS SAFE – AND THE ERUPTION'S OVER. GUESS OUR WORK'S DONE, VIRGIL!
F.A.B., SCOTT! AND NOW WE REALLY CAN GO HOME – ALTHOUGH I RECKON THE INDIANS WILL MISS THEIR SPIRIT FROM THE SKIES!

CLASSIC COMICS

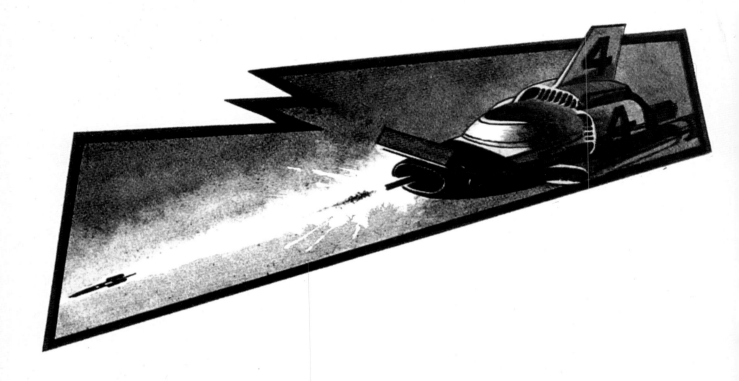

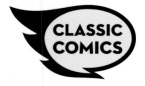

EGMONT